PERMISSION TO

LEAP

THE SIX-PHASE JOURNEY TO BRING
YOUR VISION TO LIFE

BRI SEELEY

FOREWORD BY NAVEEN JAIN

*Permission to Leap
is dedicated to everyone
who desires to answer the
call of their soul and bring
their vision to life.*

Your vision is
waiting for you!
Love&Leaps,
Robi

Contents

Contents

Contents

DOWNLOAD YOUR FREE RESOURCES

Welcome to *Permission to Leap*! Throughout this book you will find resources to support you in taking your leap in real time. The best way to experience this book is to apply the principles directly to your life to support yourself in bringing your vision to life. I created specific worksheets and meditations to help.

Access your free resources here:
http://PermissionToLeap.Today

You are also invited to join the Permission to Leap online community at bit.ly/briseeleyleap.

FOREWORD

Imagine a person who grew up poor looking to the moon for inspiration as a child, and now, as an adult, that same person is actually going to the moon in 2018.

Imagine then what everyone else can do.

Imagine what you can do.

Niels Bohr said to fellow physicist Wolfgang Pauli, "We are all agreed that your theory is crazy. The questions that divide us is whether it is crazy enough to have a chance of being correct."

We are living in the most innovative decade in human history, and I believe the next 10 years will fundamentally change the trajectory of how humanity lives. And yet, in a world where we have more access to more resources than ever before, we consistently approach our lives with a mentality of scarcity, a mindset that values things only because we believe they are scarce. We have been conditioned to believe it's someone else's job to solve our problems and create change. However, I am here to tell you that once you change your mindset from one of scarcity to a mindset of abundance, you begin to think of potentials and possibilities rather than the things that can't be done. You start to see the world in a very different way. You don't have to focus on "what is" and start focusing on "what it can be". This is when you can start to predict the future because you are creating it.

What separates those who are willing to be considered crazy for dreaming big and those who don't dream big at all is the fear of failure. I say if people don't think you're crazy, then you're not thinking big enough! Exacting change doesn't begin outside of ourselves; the change must first begin inside. It's only when you access the truth of who you are internally that you begin to realize you have everything you need externally to do all you want in this life.

It is people like Bri who are changing the world - from the inside out - and she is the only person cut out to write this book because she chose to do it. She didn't keep the idea to herself and wait for someone else to come along and write it for her. When you say something is impossible, it becomes impossible for you, not for anybody else. Bri stood up and said, "I'll do it."

But how do we do it? How do we quiet the external noise and tune in to our internal voice? I'm glad you asked, and you're already on the right track if you're holding this book in your hands. Permission to Leap is an invitation for you to boldly claim, "The life I want is possible for me," with clear steps that allow you to take action toward that life every day.

Bri's insights and guidance contained in this book will disrupt the way you think about yourself and the way you operate in the world. Your lens of scarcity will soon be replaced with a lens of abundance and everything you ever thought impossible will become possible. These steps can be assembled like Legos into your life. They can be swapped out, upgraded, replaced. It doesn't matter how big the obstacle or dream may be if you can slice it into smaller, manageable tasks then you can execute with relative ease.

When resources are in abundance, like the air we breathe, we don't live from a position of scarcity. The question is: Are you willing to make a change for yourself that can ultimately change the world we all live in? If the answer is yes, I challenge you to commit to taking your leap with the help of Permission to Leap. And along the way, remember this: It's not about simply changing your perspective or point of view; it's about altering the path you are on altogether. The biggest risk you will take in life is not doing something. So, with this book, you literally have nothing to lose!

I believe you can, and will, accomplish anything if you set your mind to it. The reason people are scared to take risks is because they don't believe in themselves. It's possible to lose the fear of failure if you continually speak to yourself with confidence, "I never fail; I pivot." Reading and executing the information contained in this book will allow you to see further and with greater clarity to actually go create your crazy, impossible vision. The future you imagine will come true, and you'll find yourself surrounded by those who believe in you because they believe in the cause.

JFK said, "We chose to go to the moon not because it's easy, but because it's hard." This isn't going to be easy, but I promise you, it will be worth it. I came to the U.S. in 1982 with just $5 in my pocket. In 2018, I am going to the moon. Won't you join me on this journey to make the impossible possible?

Naveen Jain

A NOTE TO YOU

WARNING

You cannot unknow the information contained in this book. As Morpheus explained to Neo in *The Matrix*, while revealing a red pill and a blue pill simultaneously in each palm, "You take the blue pill and the story ends [meaning, you close this book]. You wake up in your bed and believe whatever you want to believe. You take the red pill [meaning, you choose to turn the page], you stay in Wonderland and I show you how deep the rabbit hole goes."

What you're about to read will cause you to see everything in a new way.

WHAT IS A LEAP?

There are not enough people in the world taking leaps. To leap is to attempt something new, knowing the outcome cannot be proven. The desire to leap is often marked by either a deep unsettling discomfort, indicating the circumstances you find yourself in are not right, or by an inner knowing that there is more available to you than your current reality.

Plenty of people talk about taking leaps and imagine "one day"—one day when the magic synchronicity of perfection removes all issues, barriers, obstacles, situations, circumstances, and resistance to finally allow them to say "yes" to their deepest desires. They dream about that day, when all of life is aligned, when the heavens open, the seas part, and everything clicks magically into place without fear. You know these people. You might even be one of them.

Well, I'm sorry to tell you, but that day will never arrive. Tomorrow is a magical, mystical land where dreams go to die. If you wake up every day for the rest of your life saying, "One day," or relying on tomorrow, your life will end without ever truly beginning.

Maybe you're leaving a job or a relationship. Maybe you're changing careers entirely or entering retirement. Maybe you've decided to start or close a business, or you're relocating, or you're facing a serious medical issue. Maybe it's just a simple understanding that what you're currently experiencing in life isn't working, and it's time for something new. No matter what your story is, this book was written to support you in taking your leap with ease and grace.

WHY DID I WRITE THIS BOOK?

I wrote this book because of yoga, a move to Los Angeles, a car accident, and a business closure. I wrote this book because I have chosen—and been forced—to make a series of big leaps in my life that have changed everything about the way I start each day and how I approach life and business. Unfortunately, there are not enough people committing to the leap that their heart and soul desperately craves, and I am determined to change that.

A lot of fear and hesitation are wrapped up in taking big leaps because not enough people are talking about the reality of this process. The actual phases of a leap, as well as the treasure chest of emotions experienced during a leap, have become a precious commodity, a secret locked away, the key swallowed for safekeeping. I can't tell you why this knowledge has been safeguarded—everyone has their reasons to keep it to themselves—but I'm picking the lock and giving you access.

More importantly, I'm giving you permission to utilize this long-held secret in your own life. The more you know about the reality of leaping, the more confident and secure you'll feel in deciding to leap. You'll embody a deep trust in the unknown path before you, and you won't quit mid-leap.

This book is for those ready to make the leap and those who are still hesitant about it. I believe that once you see and understand what's involved in the process of bringing your vision to life, the decision to say "yes" to your leap will become an obvious no-brainer.

Permission to Leap is a step-by-step guide to take you through the entire leap process from the day of your first commitment to the day your feet land on the other side. It is a vulnerable and actionable outline of what to expect when you leap and how to handle the emotions and fears that surface. It is also a source of support while you build the resiliency to leap over and over again.

At the end of this book—because I know you've chosen to take the red pill and turn the page—I promise you will be infused with confidence to commit to your leap and will proudly declare, "Screw tomorrow. I'm saying 'yes' today. I refuse to wait any longer."

Love + Leaps,
Bri

Part One:

PREPARING FOR YOUR LEAP

1. Basic Understandings

In order for you to get the most out of this book, I want to start with the foundational understandings this book is built on and invite you into some opportunities that will heighten your experience here and beyond. I've also included a glossary (in the back of the book) for your reference, in case some of the language I'm using is brand new to you.

~

Because yoga allows me to connect with myself, I find starting the morning with this ritual sets my energy in the right direction for the entire day ahead. One morning in 2016, as the sun was rising, I stepped onto my yoga mat in the space between my kitchen and living room. I faced the patio to see the hummingbirds enjoying their sugary breakfast, brought my hands together over my heart, and in the quiet of being present, I heard a very clear message: "You are the divine intersection of Spirit and Earth."

It caught me off guard. It was weird. Where was this thought coming from?

Every time I stepped onto my yoga mat after that particular morning, the phrase would repeat, over and over again, morning after morning, "You are the divine intersection of Spirit and Earth."

It was time to investigate.

My search began with a simple breath to settle my energy while I focused my conscious awareness and attention inside my body. I allowed a peaceful calm to ripple throughout my muscles, and with my palms held together over my heart, I asked, "Show me. Show me what being the divine intersection of Spirit and Earth means. Reveal to me why this phrase keeps coming so persistently into my life. What do I need to learn from this?"

My eyes fluttered closed as I raised my left leg, settling into tree pose with my hands still hovering in prayer over my heart. "Show me," I asked again.

I took a deep breath, and another, and then another. In my third breath, the answer trickled through.

I could feel a light, sparkling energy moving into my body through my head, down into my throat, wrapping around my heart, and moving into my belly and out of my feet. At the same time, my focus was drawn to one of my cats rubbing against my standing leg, my skin warming from the sun's rays spilling in through the window, and the soft sounds of my spa music playing in my ears.

Oh, I think I get it. A spectrum popped into my head:

| Spirit | You | Earth |

For a moment, I could feel myself directly in the center of this spectrum, experiencing both the seen and the unseen simultaneously. This mix of energy swirled through my body as I relaxed into the tangible reality of my present moment. I was a bridge between the invisible, Universal (spirit) energy flowing through all things and the physical world in which we reside.

I am a spirit, living in a human experience, and so are *you*.

What does that mean?

On one end of the spectrum is the spirit aspect of ourselves, which I will refer to as the Spiritual World. In this world are the things we cannot see or touch: faith, trust, magic, synchronicity, energy, etc. On the other end of the spectrum is the human aspect of ourselves, which I will refer to as the Physical World. In this world are the things we can see and touch: situations, circumstances, experiences, jobs, people, etc.

The majority of the world's population lives and operates solely on the human end of the spectrum, which means our lives are dictated by what we can see and touch. Our lives are constantly defined by our external situations and experiences because they are here right now. We can see them. We can touch them. They are our "reality." We forget what else is available to us because we rely solely on our five senses to determine what's real or not.

What I learned that morning during my yoga practice, and what I continue to learn every day, is that while our world and culture reinforces the idea that we are "meaningless specks in an indifferent Universe," (*thanks Dr. Strange*) our actual reality is much different from this. You and I exist on this spectrum of Spirit and Earth. In every moment, we have an opportunity to access both the seen and the unseen because our human existence is a combination of both.

I invite you to consider that your external reality is not the entire picture available to you. Would you be willing, if only for the duration of this book, to approach this process openly to discover and allow yourself to balance on this spectrum?

A lot of the concepts I touch upon cannot be experienced through your five senses. Why not? As of right now, your leap is pure energy—it is thought and emotion—and it will remain so for the first two-thirds of this process. Energy cannot be touched, smelled, tasted, seen, or heard, so leaps are about turning that energy into a tangible reality. It is this ability to believe in and trust the Spiritual World that allows your Physical World to shift, making way for you to create your vision and realize your leap.

In order to leap, it is critical that you change your perspective, actions, and beliefs. If you do what you've always done and believe what you've always believed, you will continue to create and experience the same things over and over and over again. If you wish to create something new in your life, you need a new way of being.

I will go deeper into this throughout the book, but for now, recognize where you currently allot your time and energy on this spectrum. Are you more focused on tangible reality, in the Physical World? Or do you approach life from a place of possibility, in the Spiritual World? This is an opportunity for you to get in touch with and become aware of where you are on the Spirit to Earth continuum.

In full transparency, I was curious about the Spiritual World for six years before I received this message on my mat. During that time, I explored meditation, yoga, reiki, and other modalities to develop a relationship with spirituality. (Don't worry; I'm not saying you need to practice for six years to trust in this unseen energy.) I've experienced multiple messages, inspiration, and guidance leading up to this moment, and you will as well when you begin to trust and access this energy on a regular and consistent basis.

YOUR CHOICE TO EXPERIENCE THIS BOOK

A second invitation, as you read this book, is to consider how you want to experience the content and activities you will learn. When it comes to responding to experiences, three types of people exist in the world: Spectators, Participants, and Creators.

To help you fully visualize this concept, imagine you're at the beach. The sky is clear and blue; it's a gorgeous, sunny day. The sand is warm under your feet. The water flows onto the shore and recedes again in a very predictable pattern.

As you sit on your towel, soaking up the rays, you look to your left and notice someone standing at the edge of the shore, gazing out at the ocean. They're close enough to feel the breeze, but they stand back far enough so the water never reaches them. They observe the flow of the waves, but they never actively contact the water. This is a Spectator.

Spectators will read this book, but they will fail to apply any of the concepts to their lives. They will experience this as an information-gathering session. The words will pass over them, and they will not do anything with them, effectively "in one ear, out the other."

Spectators will approach this book with a closed energy, refusing to allow any of the content to permeate or transform their life experience. This will play out in their thoughts: "This is nice for her, but it will not work for me," or, "My situation or circumstance cannot be changed. I'm stuck with the cards I've been dealt."

Back on the beach, you look to your right and observe another beachgoer. They are standing on the foamy, bubbly part of the shore where the waves are breaking. They're allowing the surf to wash over their feet and ankles, but they don't get any closer to the water. After a few moments of this, they turn around and return to their towel. This is a Participant.

Participants will read the book, consider the concepts, and maybe apply one or two of them, but they will then revert to life as usual. They will get it, the fire within will begin to surge, but at some point, one of two things will happen:

1. Things will get difficult. They'll get into the first phase or two of the leap process (right around the time when things begin to look like they're falling apart, they're experiencing resistance from the people in their life, and their fears begin getting louder), and they'll opt out because, let's face it, none of us like to be uncomfortable. We would all prefer everything to be sunshine and roses every day, in every way. Participants are not 100 percent committed, and when even the smallest discomfort presents itself, they'll choose to return to the safe, normal, comfortable life.

2. Or life will take over. Everything else will begin to take priority, the busy-trap will become their way of life, and they'll allow their leap to fall to the wayside. They'll want to prioritize their leap, but excuse after excuse will pop up: everything from why now is not the right time to something unexpected coming up, to needing

more information before making a decision, to how they have too much going on, to why it's not actually that important.

Participants are open to the transformation and the process, but their skepticism gets in the way. They will say they believe in the principles but refuse to embody and live by them. They'll learn the materials but fail to apply them fully to create maximum transformation.

Again, back on the beach and from your towel, you look straight ahead and watch as someone runs headfirst into the ocean. They surface in the distance, bobbing up and down with the waves. They allow their body to follow the natural movement of the water, before diving back under and emerging on the shore, dripping wet with a huge smile on their face. This is a Creator.

Creators will read the book, apply every principle, write about their experiences and epiphanies, share and discuss the book with friends, and then reread it to make sure they didn't miss anything. Creators are the ones who go *all-in*. These are the ones unwilling to continue life as-is, the ones unwilling to accept their current circumstances as truth and unable to dim desires any longer. They are open and willing to respond, and they make a full commitment to their leap as non-negotiable, top priority.

Not only are Creators prepared to believe in the possibility of their leap, they will do whatever it takes to embody this belief so deeply that even when they're unsure of the path, they show up and take inspired action.

The Creators are going to get the most out of this process because greatness happens through dedication, commitment, and tenacity.

With this invitation, I ask you to decide how you will experience and engage with this book. Will you choose to be a Spectator, a Participant, or a Creator?

I, _____, am committed to experiencing

this process as a _____.

SETTING YOUR INTENTION

In addition to this preliminary commitment, I invite you to set an intention for your experience with this book.

What is an intention? An intention is a clear, positive statement aiming toward an outcome you desire to experience or create. Intentions differ from goals in that they address the journey or path rather than the end point. Stating your intention provides you with an idea of how to act and how to be in the present moment.

When you set your intention about how you want to experience this book, when you know your commitment to being a Spectator, Participant, or Creator, you are more likely to achieve this. Being aware of and acting from your intentions will make you more effective in creating the results you desire and achieving the goals you set for yourself.

Take a moment and get clear on your purpose for reading this book. Is it a simple knowledge-gathering expedition? Or do you desire to not only learn but also apply the tools contained here to support you in leaping successfully into your future?

If you're not fully sure how to answer these questions, that's OK! Stating the simple intention, "I am open to fully receiving the information in this book," is a great way to get started!

Take a few minutes to write your answers to these questions before moving any deeper into the book.

PATIENCE, MY LOVE

We live in a world filled with instant gratification and overnight success. You want ice cream at midnight on a Tuesday? Order it online, and it will arrive in fifteen minutes. You want to increase your social media following? Purchase it. You want to go on a date? Swipe right.

Anything and everything we desire can now be delivered or bought almost instantaneously.

Well, nearly anything and everything.

Prepare yourself courageously for what's to come. Fully executing the leap process takes time, attention, and commitment. If you desire to do big things in the world, make an impact, and ignite change in your life and/or the world around you, there is no "instant." It is a process.

I began my journey as an entrepreneur at the age of twenty-three, fresh off the plane from Italy where I completed my Master's Diploma in Arte della Moda (Fashion as Art). I was bright-eyed and naive, itching to be discovered and convinced that I would become an instant hit like the next Justin Bieber song.

Design after design, collection after collection, runway show after runway show. I wanted it now. I was constantly fixated on why it wasn't happening. Each event I attended and each runway show where I exhibited, I walked in believing that would be my defining moment when everything would change. And when my expectations were not met, I spun into disappointment and resentment.

Looking back now, I was full-on Veruca Salt-ing my way through my business:

I want the world,
I want the whole world.
Give it to me now!
And if I don't get the things I am after
I'm going to scream!
I want the works,
I want the whole works!
Presents and prizes and sweets and surprises
in all shapes and sizes,
And now!
I don't care how. I want it now!

I showed up in my business every day from this place of impatience, focusing on what wasn't happening and why things weren't unfolding quickly enough. I was so consumed that I was unable to recognize when things were going right; I was incapable of celebrating the small victories. A momentary, "OK, that happened. What's next?" was the only gratitude I employed. My impatience and desire for instant gratification had me so heavily in mental fail-mode that after a few years, it brought about the end of my business.

When that happened, I knew I needed to do things differently if I wanted to create a sustainable life and business for myself. I knew that if I were to leap into another venture constantly craving a quick fix, the same thing would happen over and over again.

While allowing myself to grieve the loss of my first business, I began to investigate my feelings and beliefs tied to my impatience. I became incredibly aware of the thoughts in my mind, which led me to recognize how little I believed in abundance and how rarely I demonstrated gratitude. And I learned that by seeking to be discovered or labeled the next "It Designer," I was putting my success in the hands of others.

> "Change happens when we start retraining certain behaviors, thoughts and emotions, and begin executing new thoughts, behaviors and emotions."
> Dr. Joe Dispenza

As a result of my willingness to uncover and analyze my behaviors, thoughts, and emotions, I was able to create a new trajectory for myself. I cleared out what wasn't working and made a commitment to change my behaviors, thoughts, and emotions to be in alignment with my definition of success so that I could create it for myself, instead of waiting for someone to give it to me.

This process resulted in the most profound changes I have ever experienced. It was this consistent, repeated commitment to shift my life and my mind, day after day after day, and releasing the need for immediate results that created the book now in your hands.

Leaping is about showing up again and again, regardless of whether it looks like things are going your way or not. Leaping requires continued faith that even when you cannot see or touch the outcome immediately, it's coming. Leaping asks you to exercise consistent patience when things don't move as quickly as you desire. Leaping challenges you to trust in the process and not bail mid-leap because it looks like your life is falling apart around you.

Leaping is also an opportunity to remind us to be easier on ourselves. Remember to shower yourself with loads of compassion for deciding to take this journey. Remind yourself you need space to breathe. Prioritize your self-care and nourishment. Exercise patience with yourself and the process.

More than anything: Keep showing up. Every day. No matter what.

2. Two Worlds Collide

I live straddling two worlds, much like the spectrum I presented at the beginning. I live in the Physical World, but I also live very much in the Spiritual World.

What's the difference?

The Physical World is the material world in which we all live. It's the world in which our five senses (touch, taste, sight, smell, sound) perceive what's real, and it is always temporary.

The Spiritual World is everything we can't tangibly perceive with our senses (although we can feel it through what is often referred to as a "sixth sense."). It is our faith, emotions, beliefs, thoughts, intentions, consciousness, intuition, higher power, etc. The Spiritual World relies on an unending supply of Universal energy that, as we know from high school physics class, can be neither created nor destroyed; it becomes eternal.

There was a switch in the history of the world where our species began to value the Physical World more than the Spiritual World, a shift primarily associated with the Scientific Revolution. During this period of time, a very specific view of reality permeated the world, one characterized by observable and verifiable facts, one that drew the conclusion that real and true things must be confirmed by science and anything existing outside this was hallucinatory or imaginary.

The Scientific Revolution emphasized we must use our surroundings and circumstances to define our realities because they are observable and verifiable. After centuries of this thought process being the forefront of Western society and culture, we now live in a world where we base almost every decision we make on what we perceive as reality in our Physical

World. We allow these "facts" to dictate our moods, decide our successes, and prevent us from trusting in the Spiritual World.

Defining yourself by what lives outside you and relying on it to complete you does not work. It is the recipe for victimhood and requires everything in the Physical World to be perfect before you take action on your vision, before you feel satisfied or fulfilled by your life. When you run your life constantly focused on what is external, you remain in fear of the unknown, resistant to building trust in yourself, and you allow others to dictate your worth and success.

We've been taught all wrong. The Physical World is perceived as the most important indicator of our place in the world, our ability to pursue our dreams, and our worthiness. We've been defined by situations, circumstances, and consumerism for far too long.

This explains why leaps get super tricky for us. Leaps are built on our understanding of, trust in, and connection to the Spiritual World. It is this connection with the unseen that creates our Physical World surroundings and circumstances, not the other way around. In order to leap, you must place more weight in the possibility of the Spiritual World rather than in the current state of your Physical World, which is where the terms "blind faith" and "leap of faith" come in. It's about finding a part of yourself that is more willing to believe in and trust the possibility of what you desire, and less willing to continue perpetuating the spiral of your present perspective.

Think about it. Leaps consist of a combination of energy, thoughts, beliefs, faith, and emotions; the majority of every leap requires trust in things you cannot see or touch. So it is the importance our society places on the Physical World that keeps us from leaping.

We associate our reality with the tangibility of the Physical World—I can see and touch it, therefore it is real—which then leads us to a secondary conclusion: If I cannot see or touch it, it is not real.

But our eyesight deceives us. By placing too much importance on our senses, we fail to remember that everything we desire is right in front of our faces. It is the lack of faith, connection, and trust that keeps us from seeing what it is we desire manifested in the Physical World.

We've all heard the phrase, "I'll believe it when I see it," an all-too-common saying that leads us to the understanding that the sequence of events is: sight then belief.

Which is completely wrong. The statement is backwards.

The actual sequence of events does not run from sight to belief. Instead, it moves from belief into sight. If you don't believe in what you desire within the Spiritual World, you'll never see it in the Physical World. Leaping means trusting the relationship will work out, your ideal job will come up in your job searches, new income will present itself, or you'll find your new home—well before you receive confirmation of those things in the Physical World.

Belief, trust, and faith in the Spiritual World come first. Results and proof in the Physical World come second. The creation of your life starts inside you and then moves to the outer world. Not the other way around. Faith does not mean waiting for evidence.

Think about it: the act of any leap is to turn possibility into tangibility. So of course you won't be able to have proof before you leap. There isn't any proof to be had considering it's still just pure energy, an idea not yet birthed into the Physical World.

Yet we continue to attach our ability to believe in our visions to some sort of Physical World proof. We still require it to be present before we believe in the possibility.

This concept is not conditional; it's universal. You don't get to selectively choose which intangible things to first believe in.

Can you imagine applying this concept to the air we breathe? I can't see it, but I continue to breathe in and out with a deep trust that air will be there to fill my lungs. If I needed proof the air would be there before I took a breath, I would die very quickly.

What about the gravity that keeps us connected to the planet? You trust it to be there every day, don't you? Yet you can't see it. It's not tangible in the Physical World. We can't pick up gravity as if it were a mug, touch it, and say, "This is real," just as we can't pick up our thoughts and ideas.

What's the difference between trusting in the air you breathe and the gravity that holds our world together and believing in your dreams or creating your desires? What is the gap for you in having steadfast faith in your leap? You already possess the ability to trust in things you cannot see.

Maybe we trust in air and gravity because we've been told again and again that they are real. We're also told again and again we need to be "practical," we need to follow the well-worn path in front of us: finish school, get a job, save money, buy a house, etc. Now, I'm not saying it's a bad path. I'm just saying it may not be your path. It's certainly not mine.

Instead of waiting for evidence that your ideas, dreams, and vision are possible, why not treat them as if they were the air you breathe and the gravity that keeps you connected to the Earth?

This is an opportunity to stop waiting because if you're sitting around expecting proof it's safe to leap to show up on your doorstep, well I suggest you get comfortable. You're going to be waiting for a very long time. Faith does not mean waiting for evidence.

DEVELOP FAITH IN WHAT YOU CANNOT SEE

I've always been a little (OK, maybe a lot) obsessed with things invisible to our human eye. I remember sitting in the back of my mom's Chevy Chevette as a child, staring out at the night sky, imagining what was past it. What existed beyond the sky? There had to be more.

I would allow my mind to venture past the confines of our planet and into the vastness of the Universe. Hours of staring into our solar system led me to asking question after question with no foreseeable answers. What was out there in this unending darkness above me? What existed before our planet was even a thing? Where did it all lead?

Maybe I had been watching too much of *The Never Ending Story*. Or maybe I was onto something.

Looking back on it now, I know I was trying to access things I couldn't see with my eyes; things my human brain couldn't possibly comprehend. This yearning to know what existed beyond our Physical World became an itch I couldn't scratch.

My childhood was fraught with random emotional outbursts—evenings getting out of the bathtub with water dripping all over the floor to match the tears pouring out of my eyes, and a complete inability to put into words what was bothering me. All I could manage between the sobs was a steady stream of, "I don't know, I don't know, I don't know." I yearned for more than the Physical World could provide, and yet I knew nothing more than what I could see. Crying was the only tool I had to respond to the friction between my heart and my environment.

It wasn't until decades later that I would begin to understand these intense emotions and process the insane discomfort I experienced as a child. What was most interesting was that my heart knew all along and was sending me hints, but my humanity and my mind could not process the unseen Spiritual World. No matter how amazing my friends and family were (and believe me, they were truly, truly amazing), I always felt like I didn't fit. Despite the love and support, there was a constant, though low, hum of disharmony around and inside me.

My discomfort was insatiable. The things I could see in my life—family, friends, experiences, travel, etc.—were supposed to be making me happy, but they weren't filling me up. I was never able to put my feelings into words, and I constantly wanted more, even when the Physical World was providing me everything I could ever ask for. In addition to confusion and dissonance, my guilt was palpable. Why was it that I was so blessed with immense love, security, adventures, and Barbies up the wazoo, yet I couldn't be happy?

I was given anything I asked for. I always got to decide the dinner plans. I snuggled my mom every night on the couch. I played Parcheesi and did puzzles after school with Grandma. I went to work with Mom in the afternoons, where her coworkers and employees showered me with love. I had frequent play dates with friends. What was wrong with me? Why couldn't these things be enough to satisfy me?

I didn't know. All I knew was the ache for something different was there, standing beside me constantly. Because I didn't know—and especially because I couldn't see—what was wrong, I retreated inward and used books and movies to escape.

My obsession with *The Wizard of Oz* grew and grew. Not only was it an epic movie, but I couldn't wait for the day when my world turned to color, the day a tornado would scoop me up (which was not much of a stretch, considering I lived in Minnesota) and take me to my own Munchkinland— or New York City. I would have been happy with that too.

In the sixth grade, I read ten times more books in one quarter than any other student in my class. I preferred to stay indoors and read by myself than go play with the neighbors. Even when I was at friends' houses, I would withdraw from playing with them to be by myself.

I found I could ease the friction in my heart and focused inward. Now, of course, at that time I didn't have the knowledge to fully understand what was going on, but looking back on it and my experiences from returning to Minnesota since I left, it's clear to me my dissatisfaction was a direct result of my Physical and Spiritual Worlds being out of alignment, and my inability to do anything about it.

It wasn't until my mid-twenties, when I began to explore the Spiritual World through meditation, yoga, prayer, and visualization, things started to make sense. I experienced a calm inside my heart, the calm I had been trying to create during my entire childhood but didn't have the tools or knowledge to access. For the first time in my life, I found a sense of peace that allowed me to stop running away from life and start creating it.

"So we fix our eyes not on what is seen,
but on what is unseen, since what is seen is temporary,
but what is unseen is eternal."
2 Corinthians 4:18

Our world, solar system, and multiverse can be very tangible. Everywhere we look, we're encouraged to stay immersed in the tangibility of our "reality," yet the majority of what we experience in our daily lives (everything down to the air we breathe!) cannot be seen, touched, or experienced by our five senses.

What exists past our eyesight is infinitely more powerful than the reality that rules most of us day in and day out but we're not taught to trust it. Think about it. Everything in the Physical World is temporary. It comes and goes. It's born and it dies. Yet everything in the Spiritual World is eternal.

When you continue to believe only in your current "reality," you place yourself in a bubble, a perspective that will keep you from tapping into the limitless energy of possibility and will continue to play out the same unending cycles over and over and over again. We become victims to our present "realities" and forget the power we hold when we place the majority of importance in the Physical World.

"[People are] so hypnotized by their environment that
most people surrender and live their life in mediocrity.
And they may live that life and.... their desire may never
really rise to the surface. But if it does rise to the surface
and they ask themselves if there is something more - their
old concepts of how they viewed their life
and the world start to fall apart."
Joe Dispenza

While our culture places a heavy importance on practical planning and using our current perspectives to create the future, I'm inviting you into something new. Placing considerable emphasis on your present perspective will only continue to create more of the same in your life. What if you were to release the significance you place on the Physical World, where you'll only keep repeating what you know, and you begin to place more significance on the Spiritual World, so as to tap into the expansiveness of what is possible for your desires?

You will never be able to see the entire path or the obstacles before you commit to your leap. In every leap is an element of the unknown and the intangible because leaps require you to turn the energy of possibility into tangibility. And that equation cannot go in the opposite direction.

DO YOU CREATE OR DO YOU RESPOND?

When we continuously fall into this trap of focusing on the "realities" of our Physical World, we enter into an unending cycle of constantly responding to stimuli we likely have no control over, instead of creating what it is we desire. In this response cycle, our thoughts, actions, and beliefs are completely dependent on external measures.

It was a beautiful, stereotypical Los Angeles morning in mid-March. I was free of my day job for nearly a year, and while I still had a lot to figure out about my life and future, I was feeling particularly good that morning.

I was coming off of having completed a three-day workshop the weekend before, and for a rare moment, I felt like I was in the flow of life as I drove into my office. The sun was warm on my skin. I had a smile on my face, and I couldn't help but jam out in my car to the sounds of No Doubt.

I was sitting at a stoplight in my little Pontiac hatchback behind a large SUV. I saw the light turn to green and watched the SUV accelerate in front of me. I looked to the left briefly as I tapped my accelerator pedal lightly, then turned back to find that the SUV braking to turn without using their turn signal and knew my immediate, hard brake wasn't going to stop me in time.

In an instant, the entire front end of my car crumpled before my eyes, with me inside. My Physical World went from flow and joy to despair and fear in an instant.

After checking in with the other driver and realizing that, while the cosmetic damage was shocking, neither of us were hurt ... I sat on the sidewalk and cried. And cried. And cried.

You see, I had just signed a contract with a coach the night before with a commitment to pay her $25,000 (a contract I could not possibly execute successfully given my reality at the time). I didn't have any foreseeable, consistent income sources. My unemployment had run out. I couldn't get a job in the marketplace because I was too ambitious and therefore unemployable. And, as much as I didn't want to admit it, my fashion business wasn't working. There was no feasible way I'd be able to support myself and afford to keep the brand going.

Add to this the fact I had just totaled my car without the proper insurance to cover it. Well, let's just say that my tears were completely justified. The weight of life had become too much to bear. Given the perspective of what was before me, I had no feasible option for success.

My reality in that moment was incredibly bleak. Not only could I not afford my current expenses, but I would be taking on an additional expense with the coaching contract and adding a car payment to the mix as well.

As I sat crying on the sidewalk, my shoulders slumped and my head in my hands, waiting for a tow truck, my first response was to call the coach to bail and walk away from my commitment. With everything racing through my mind, how could I not?

From where I sat, I mapped out two options:

> 1. I could respond to my life circumstances and allow the limitations of my situation to dictate my next moves. I could walk away from the thing my heart and soul had said "yes" to because I couldn't possibly see how it could all work itself out and abandon my faith,

turning my back on a truth only felt, a truth that didn't exist in the Physical World.

This was the answer society, my community, and my rational brain would have led me to choose. Based on the circumstances currently available to me, there was no way it could be a good idea to stay in the commitment to the coaching contract. Looking at it from this angle only resulted in fear, confusion, and despair, prompting me to believe it wasn't a possibility and should be discounted as an option—because I could not conceivably make decisions about my future without tangible evidence.

2. Or I could create what I wanted, say "yes," and remain committed without seeing any proof that what I desired was possible. I had the opportunity at my fingertips to trust deeply the Spiritual World was supporting my decision. It was a chance to live past the dissatisfaction and frustration I was experiencing in the Physical World and create something new for myself.

My reality was option 1 did not feel good. Turning my back on the possibility at my fingertips felt more like a dead end than continuing forward in the uncertainty of how my financial situation would work out. If I didn't invest and set myself up to find a new path, I would just keep spiraling in the victimhood of what I could see before me.

On the other hand, if I did invest, I would be forcing myself to find a new path and set myself up for a life greatly expanded.

Was I willing to put my faith in an outcome that didn't "make sense"? Or was I going to succumb to relinquishing my desires based on the information currently perceivable to my senses?

As I prepared to write this book, I spent much of my time this year reflecting on all my leaps. I was recently catching up with a close friend and confidante, Jack, who was by my side during one of the major leaps in my life, my leap to leave Washington and relocate to Los Angeles which you'll learn more about as you continue reading. I brought the conversation back to a night in 2012 when we were standing around a bonfire under the full moon. That night, in circle with our community, he said to me, "You have the deepest and strongest faith of anyone I've ever met."

I heard the statement at the time, but never fully received or processed the comment. It wasn't until our conversation five years later that I finally inquired, "What do you mean by that?"

"Well, when you moved to Los Angeles, the 'correct' option was to not go. You were experiencing so much success with your career, your business, your relationships, and your life HERE—and all the sudden you packed everything up and left. From a traditional perspective, it didn't 'make sense' for you to let it all go and start from scratch."

Jack continued, "But I think that's what makes you so powerful, Bri. Despite the uncertainty and doubts, you chose to focus on the possibility of what could come to be and trusted that you would be supported. You don't need to see the results to know that you're on the right path. Instead, you consistently trust that you are being guided, you're open to listening, and you release your control on the situation. You're willing to see things differently. You're willing to see past what is and explore what could be if you only believed in the possibility of it."

The life we see and experience every day is only the smallest sliver of what is available to us. Jack's reflection of me was a great reminder of what I know to be true but sometimes forget, since it's not staring me in the face.

The application of this consistent trust in my vision, and myself has been the top contributing factor to success in my life. In addition to everything in the aforementioned paragraphs, my ability to approach my daily life from the energy of possibility has shifted everything from who I have become to what I've been able to create. Every leap I have committed to comes with an accompanying question of faith: Do I trust in what's to come without being able to see it? You will face this question during the journey of your leap as well. Will you continue to respond to what's in front of you, or will you choose to create what it is you desire?

If you haven't guessed by now, I made the commitment to lean on my faith after that car accident. I got home from the auto shop and went straight to my yoga mat where I proceeded to ugly cry for an hour. I cried away the anger tied to the decisions I made that got me to that point. I cried away the fear of the unknown path before me. I cried away the anxiety, the disappointment, and the regret ... until there was nothing left to cry in that moment.

And then I picked myself up off the floor, popped a gluten-free frozen pizza into the oven, and danced to *Shake It Off* three times in my living room. All while my cats stared at me as if I were a madwoman.

As I inhaled my pizza, I found I was faced with a decision.

> 1. I could let my day be completely ruined, even though it was still before noon. I could wallow in a hole of my own creation and continue to allow the "reality" of my present circumstance shit all over me.

> 2. Or I could allow this to be a great day. I could be in gratitude for my and the other driver's safety, for the fact I walked away without a scratch, bump, or bruise from an accident that totaled my car, and for my fortitude to keep moving forward.

Sitting in the backseat of a Lyft just thirty minutes later, I explained to the driver what an amazing day I was experiencing. I shared with him how I had totaled my car and why it was turning into the best day I'd had in a long time. He thought I was completely crazy and even asked me what I had been smoking.

How could I have totaled my car a few hours prior and be sitting in the backseat of his car with a huge smile on my face, a full heart, and a positive outlook?

Because I leaned on my faith. I refused to see it as a negative experience. I didn't know why quite yet, but I trusted it all happened for a reason. And even though I couldn't yet see the silver lining in the moment, it didn't mean it wasn't there.

By relying on my inner faith and defining what was true for me in the Spiritual World, I created results in the Physical World that were aligned with my inner state of being.

After working at my office for a few hours that same day, I walked to the nearby taco truck to grab lunch. I looked down as I walked back into my office, and sitting in the middle of the doorway was a business card that read, "We Buy Cars." That business card had not been there when I initially arrived to the office, but it was the nudge I needed to support me in deciding once and for all to let go of my car and sell it for parts, rather than paying more than it was worth to fix it.

Leaning into the supportive energy of friends, I made two phone calls to secure my new car in under six hours—and it wasn't just any car. It was a car I had been aligning myself with for several months—leather seats, Bluetooth-compatible, a much smoother ride. A short forty-eight hours after the accident, I was on a lot in the valley signing paperwork on my brand-new Lexus.

More than anything, my decision to rely on my faith and continue with the coaching contract was validated. In just seven months of working with my coach, I closed my fashion brand and created my current business. I can unequivocally say this book would not exist in your hands if I had remained a victim to my Physical World perspective at the time of my accident.

There will always be unknown elements to life. Our humanity craves to minimize the elements of the unknown to create certainty, predictability, and safety. What I'm inviting you into is a comfort with the unknown and an excitement for the possibilities it holds, rather than discounting it and viewing it through a negative lens.

We'll never fully eliminate or avoid the unseen. So instead of fighting against it, the best way to handle it is to cultivate the inner strength and stamina to be in harmony with it. How do we shift from a predominant perspective and importance in the Physical World into a perspective primarily rooted in the Spiritual World?

One way is to exercise your faith in small ways. If you already have faith in the air you breathe and the gravity that is all around, it is completely possible for you to also have faith in your dreams. Begin to identify things, experiences, and people that you already have faith in. What do you trust in this moment? Look at what unifies the things on this list—is there a thread of commonality that ties them all together? If you can identify what you currently have faith in, it can help you expand your mind and beliefs into other areas where you could also have faith.

Another way is to begin to access the Spiritual World on a consistent basis. In Chapter 4, I will guide you through creating a daily practice to build and strengthen your relationship with the unknown through meditation, visualization, gratitude, and more. Maintaining this daily connection will not only open up an entirely new world to you, it will also help increase your confidence in making decisions from a broader perspective.

More than anything else though, you need to develop a relationship with your intuition so that it becomes second nature.

LET YOUR INTUITION BE YOUR GUIDE

Intuition is the only thing that will lead you down your path. The word *intuition* comes from the Latin *intuir,* which appropriately means "knowledge from within." We all possess the ability to tap into our intuition; we've just covered it up and buried it for so long the connection has weakened.

If our intuition is a natural part of who we are in the world, how does it possibly get covered up? Well, it's due to a lot of what I've been mentioning already: It's not concrete or tangible; therefore, we're taught not to trust it. The Internet is fraught with article after article about how intuition is not real. The top search results for "don't trust your intuition" include a *Harvard Business Review* article referring to intuition as "dangerously unreliable" (Bonabeau 2003), a Forbes article stating that our "intuition deceives us" (Blakeley 2010), and the article "When Intuition Misfires" from the American Psychiatric Association that tells us our intuition "often fails us" (Greer 2005).

Deductive reasoning is given much more weight in our culture. We're encouraged to be logical and rational: Start where you are, weigh the pros and cons, forecast and analyze all possible outcomes, and choose the least risky option with the highest probability for success. After all, this keeps your perspective focused in the Physical World.

Sometimes our logic and our intuition align. Those moments are magical and make our decision process a whole lot easier. But what about the times they don't align? What about the decisions we face where our intuition is trying to steer us to the right, but our logic keeps screaming to turn left?

Cognitive psychologists Daniel Simons and Christopher Chabris wrote an entire book trying to convince you to use your intuition only on decisions that don't matter, such as which song to listen to on the radio and which ice cream flavor to choose. They wrote that once the decision has an objective standard of quality, logic should be the only perspective consulted in the process. We should not use intuition above analysis.

I disagree entirely.

Our intuition brings something to the table that logic misses: the element of the unknown and access to the Spiritual World. Our intuition is capable of looking past the circumstances of the present moment and connecting to the possibility of the future. It has access to more areas of understanding and various perspectives, and it taps into a deep inner knowledge that cannot be accessed in the Physical World.

Have you noticed what happens when your intuition says "no," but you logic'ed yourself into a "yes"? Maybe it was a business deal where your intuition knew the people involved were shady, but the numbers looked good so you committed ... only to find out the people on the other side were stealing from or manipulating you in some way. Maybe it was an entrepreneurial venture that just didn't feel right, but everyone you knew was having success with it … only to find out it involved a monetary buy-in or sales technique that just didn't align with your values. Maybe it was getting married when your intuition told you it was a bad idea … only to find out they were keeping a secret from you. Maybe it was feeling off when you were dating someone, but since there was no reason for you to feel off, you looked past it … only to find out later they had been cheating on you.

The right answer doesn't always make the most sense. In fact, I would say when it comes to leaps, *rarely* does the right answer make logical sense. Like my friend Jack reflected to me, the right answer was not to move to Los Angeles. It didn't make sense. Based on the proof from the Physical World, I should have stayed in Washington.

This is why intuition is such an important piece of this conversation. It is a tool that will be critical in your leap because we don't leap based on logic. Leaps require you to tap into something bigger than you can currently see. They ask you to find faith and trust in possibility. We make leaps by tuning into and being guided by the intangibility of the Spiritual World.

Stop obsessing over right and wrong. Stop asking other people for their opinions. Stop looking to what others are doing to get their results. Stop looking for quick fixes. Stop gathering more information.

In the entrepreneurial sphere, it's common to fall into the "Six Steps to Success." Or when applying for jobs, it's common to fall into the "Six Keys to a Memorable Resume/Job Interview." But trying to build your path the same way others have built theirs isn't necessarily the answer. No one else has your answers. No one else is walking your path. You must create it.

Using your intuition feels risky and scary if you're not familiar with it, but it gets easier the more you use it. It's like building a muscle.

The first step in learning to use your intuition is to begin differentiating between your "yes" feeling and your "no" feeling. These two feelings show up differently in different people, but they are always in stark contrast to each other. For example, my "yes" feels like champagne toward the bottom of my sternum. It's light, airy, and bubbly. My "no" feels like a solid, dull wall in my rib cage.

The easiest way to get a sense of these two feelings is by sitting in stillness, relaxing your mind and body, then inviting the feeling to reveal itself: "show me what *yes* feels like," followed by, "show me what no feels like." You may need to revisit this exercise again and again until you feel very clear on how each sensation shows up in your body.

Once you feel more confident recognizing these two sensations, you can start utilizing your intuition in the Physical World. I recommend beginning with decisions that have no emotional attachments. Great examples of this include choosing which avocado to purchase at the grocery store, which line to get into at Target, which route to drive/walk home, etc. Practicing with your intuition in situations not involving emotion enables you to strengthen your communication with your intuition as emotions can cloud our intuitive abilities. Keep practicing every day so your intuition becomes an automatic response in your decision-making process.

The leap into which you are about to journey is yours and yours alone. This book will give you a framework to start the exploration process, but every single person who reads this will have a different experience, uncover a different path, and find their own unique way to bring their vision into the world.

No matter what, access to this path will mainly come to you through the Spiritual World. Remember, leaps are created from possibility. Proof of your leap in the Physical World will not arrive immediately, and it definitely won't arrive before you commit to your vision.

3. Step Away from Your Comfort Zone

Let's talk about comfort zones for just a hot second. We all have one. Yours may look different from mine, but no matter what your comfort zone looks like, I can promise you one thing—it's doing you no favors. In order to move forward with your leap, it's crucial for you to understand the part that your biology plays in the leap process.

WHAT IS THE COMFORT ZONE?

The comfort zone is a psychological state in which familiarity reigns supreme. It ignites a sense of ease and a perception of being in control, which results in low levels of anxiety and stress. This psychological state creates a steady level of performance. We stay in this place to avoid any anticipated pain or perceived future discomfort.

Psychologist Dr. Judith M. Bardwick refers to this state as the "anxiety-neutral" position, while Dr. Brené Brown describes it as a state of being "where our uncertainty, scarcity and vulnerability are minimized — where we believe we'll have access to enough love, food, talent, time, admiration. Where we feel we have some control."

It's a state where you perform steadily and don't have anxiety, where things are more certain and in control, and where you don't have to be vulnerable. Tell me again why this is such a bad thing?

Well, inside your comfort zone there is no increase in performance, certainty and control are only illusions, and a lack of vulnerability leaves us numb—we simply go through the motions of life. Doesn't sound as fantastic anymore, right?

Our brains will always lead us back to our comfort zones. Why? Because our brain chemistry is designed to keep us safe, which is a great thing when we're near a hot surface or in danger, but it's not such a great thing when it comes to leaps. Our brain categorizes leaps as unsafe, and it will do everything in its power to keep us safe. That is its job. It will always convince us we need to stay where we are with what we can see, minimize uncertainty, and be in control (otherwise known as living in a bubble).

The conundrum becomes very easy to see: true growth and magic happens when we are outside this perceived safety zone, but our brains want us to go back to safety again and again. So what do we do when our heart is pleading with us to leap, but our head is screaming for safety?

"Whatever your Comfort Zone consists of, you pay a huge price for it. Life provides incredible possibilities, but you can't take advantage of them without facing pain. If you can't tolerate pain, you can't be fully alive. By staying in the Comfort Zone you end up relinquishing your most cherished dreams and aspirations."
Barry Michels, LCSW, JD

Your comfort zone is doing you no favors because it's keeping you from the greatest rewards in life. The people willing to move out of this safe zone are the ones who reach the end of life with fewer regrets, a high level of life satisfaction, and results more aligned with the desires behind their actions.

In 1908, psychologists Robert M. Yerkes and John D. Dodson conducted a study about comfort zones, stress, and anxiety (Yerkes and Dodson 1908). Their results proved that a state of comfort produced a steady plateau of performance and in order to maximize performance, humans need to experience some amount of anxiety in order to raise stress levels slightly higher than normal. But it's important to note it can't be a high level of anxiety because that produces a level of stress negatively impacting our productivity and significantly decreasing our performance. The duo used mice to learn stimulation improved performance, up to a certain level, but when that level is surpassed and too much stress is incurred, performance deteriorates.

This area between our comfort zone and complete distress is known as the space of "optimal anxiety." It is there we will experience our highest realized potential ideal for our learning and growth.

The upside of low-level and short-term stress and anxiety has been studied and explained by Dr. Richard Shelton from the Department of Psychiatry at the University of Alabama Birmingham (MacMillan 2014). The reason the optimal zone is so helpful is that it increases our concentration and focus, resulting in higher levels of productivity while helping us get into the flow. It also floods our bloodstream with immune-boosting cells and boosts our resilience to tolerate stressors.

Some examples of optimal anxiety are:

- Picking up the telephone to connect with a client, instead of sending an email;

- Using direct language to communicate instead of vaguely stepping around the issue;

- Reading a book on a subject and then enrolling in a course or training to push yourself further;

- Hiring a mentor or coach to support your expansion and shifted perspective;

- Committing to a personal training program in alignment with your physical goals;

- Developing an accountability system with a colleague involving rewards and consequences.

Each of these examples is a little scary in its own right, which triggers a slight anxiety level to get you out of your comfort zone. They require a higher level of commitment and force you to take your decisions, dreams, and needs more seriously, thus bringing you to the best place to function during your leap—just far enough, but not too far, outside your comfort zone.

THE BIOLOGY OF COMFORT

To help you understand this further, let's talk about why we're hardwired for comfort, which takes us to a time in history almost entirely driven by basic survival instincts.

We each have an internal system that keeps us safe and helps us survive. The fight-or-flight response is a physiological reaction triggered by any real or perceived harmful event, attack, or threat to our survival. This reaction is the primary way we become aware of immediate danger, filter the situation, and act quickly and in a manner most likely to ensure our survival. It requires us to make quick judgments about ourself and our tribe's safety and then act accordingly.

The issue is while our stimuli has changed throughout time, this area of our brains has not evolved with the shifts in our external environments. Over the last 25,000 years, technology has completely transformed our planet, yet we are still walking around with largely the same ability to respond to life as our cavemen ancestors did. This means any phobia or personal growth will trigger our fight-or-flight response, even when we are experiencing no real threats. Our brain does not have the capacity to differentiate actual physical danger from simple personal growth. You may be consciously thinking about applying for a new job, but your brain processes it as if you're being chased by a saber-toothed tiger. You can see where this might be an issue.

Biologically, this perception of danger (which is actually just growth occurring outside our comfort zone) triggers an unconscious physical reaction throughout our bodies. Our stress response activates the adrenaline hormone preparing us to stay and fight or to run away. When it kicks in, our heart rate and respiration rapidly increase, our senses heighten, and it can even stimulate our sweat glands—all of this because you want to expand your current state of living.

Biologists believe this triggering response is critical for the survival of our species. In fact, most animals in nature rely on this instinct every day to survive. We, on the other hand, have evolved enough we don't need a prominent fight-or-flight response, yet we haven't evolved enough for it to adjust to modern living.

Our modern interpretation and experience of stress have taken on different nuances than what they meant for our ancestors. For them, the way they interpreted and experienced stress meant literal survival in the wild. But now, our current stressors are related to relationships, occupations, our physical and emotional states, home life, etc., which (for the most part) are not do-or-die situations threatening our survival. Even so, our bodies turn on the same stress response as we are in actual danger.

Our bodies have only one stress response. Inside each of us is the nervous system of a caveman desperately trying to get by in life and cope with the modern-day stressors of our increasingly fast-paced and constantly evolving world.

What does this mean to you? Well, while your heart may view your leap as simply a new business, leaving a relationship, or changing careers, your mind is spinning your entire physical being down the rabbit hole of: We are literally dying. Right now. Run.

In 2016, a woman reached out to work with me; we'll call her Athena. Everything in Athena's life was going well: she had her dream job, a fiancé, a beautiful home, the perfect puppy, a killer business on the side, and a thriving community. Yes, Athena's life was perfect except for the fact she wanted to quit her job and run her business full-time. The problem was every time she considered quitting her job, she spun into a massive fight-or-flight response with paralyzing anxiety and a vicious cycle of assumptions, doubts, and fears.

The reality was this: Athena was already meeting her monthly financial goals for her business on the side, even though she was only working part-time on it. Consciously, she knew transitioning to full-time would enable her to devote more time to increasing her income and likely double her financial goals, yet her unconscious brain was defaulting back to the habits of her caveman ancestors.

How was it that she was already meeting her requirements to be self-employed, yet her brain was telling her it was unsafe to quit her full-time job?

She was conditioned, based on her upbringing and a previously failed business, to believe the only way to have a guaranteed, consistent income was if her paychecks were coming from someone else, which meant anything threatening this conditioning translated into sudden death—or at least, that's what her brain thought.

In order to keep her "safe," Athena's brain concocted stories and excuses about why she needed to stay in her job, why she would never meet her financial goals with her business, and perpetuated the idea she would never be enough or have enough to succeed.

Athena and I worked together for six months to redefine her beliefs about self-employment, expand her business offerings, and get clear on her deeper purpose. Toward the end of our fourth month together, she gave her notice.

Despite the pain and dissatisfaction we may experience while in our comfort zone, do you now see how getting out can be painfully difficult and why most people continue to choose their current comfort zone? Our brains trigger our bodies to go into "flight mode" and then begin to convince us of all the reasons our leap is a terrible, idiotic, worst-day-ever decision. This is what I refer to as the Inner Naysayer.

NAVIGATING YOUR INNER DIALOGUE

There are generally two areas of inner dialogue that keep us from giving ourselves permission to leap. The first is the Inner Naysayer. This is the voice in your head that judges, demeans, and generally bullies you into staying in your comfort zone. The second is Imposter Syndrome, which is a persistent feeling of inadequacy despite external proof otherwise.

Inner Naysayer

The Inner Naysayer is our brain's way of bringing us back to our comfort zone and out of perceived danger. It's like our internal fire alarm, except instead of beeping to alert us, it gets mean, judge-y, angry, and abusive. It comes at us with judgments about our character and abilities, instead of just saying, "I think you're touching something hot."

During the leap process, it's more common than not to interpret this voice as a warning to prevent us from moving forward. We give our Inner Naysayer free rein to stomp on and trample our desires in total mean-girl style—all because of a simple, biological misunderstanding. Look at Athena's story. Her Physical World was showing her she had already achieved what she set out to do, and yet her brain kept telling her she'd never make it.

Now, we don't want to get rid of this voice fully because in the moments we are actually in danger, we need it to pop in and do its job. But in order to understand when it's doing its job and when it's not fully understanding the situation, one needs to begin to observe, understand, and dissect it so this biological safety mechanism is not in control of the steering wheel of our lives.

The following are three things to support you and help you stop allowing your Inner Naysayer to automatically guide your decisions, actions, and thoughts:

STEP ONE: INCREASE AWARENESS

Notice when it is noisiest. Are there certain situations when it comes up more than other situations? Notice how the voice speaks to you. What tone or sentence structure or word choices does it use?

For me, my Inner Naysayer voice is incredibly different from my normal thoughts or my intuition. Before I started on the journey of exploring my inner landscape, I heard only one uniform voice in my mind. Since increasing my familiarity with what's happening inside me, I've learned there are different parts of each of us. My normal, passing thoughts are easy to distinguish. They don't have any importance attached to them, so they come and go without emotion. These are thoughts like, "It's time to take the garbage out," or "I need to remember milk at the grocery store."

My intuition speaks to me in short sentences, usually only a few words, and the energy around it feels very solid, as if the words were a boulder being dropped. It comes through as an absolute knowing or truth. For example, when I was in meditation in January, I heard, "You're writing a book this year," accompanied by a calm, steady, powerful feeling.

My Inner Naysayer, on the other hand, speaks to me in a faster, sometimes frantic speed. It's a relentless voice repeating over and over again, perpetually trying to convince me it's right, almost as if it talking enough will force me to listen as if it's truth simply because I'm not able to hear anything else.

STEP TWO: GET CURIOUS

Begin to ask questions to distinguish what the truth of the situation is.

"Is this a real threat?" If it is—great, then don't do it. "Real threats" mean physical danger, injuring yourself, and actual harm. Threats that are not real include making a decision without knowing the outcome, trusting your intuition, changing your mindset, expanding your container, being seen in the world, and sharing your voice.

If you can distinguish these voices from each other enough to know you aren't in any real harm and your Inner Naysayer is simply presenting itself because you're outside your comfort zone, then you are faced with a decision. Do I choose fear, or do I choose my desire to grow?

STEP THREE: REPROGRAM

I will go so far as to say when these thoughts come up, it means the exact opposite of what you think. Most people hear this voice and process it as, "This is the wrong decision. My voice is coming up because I need to steer clear of my vision." I invite you to consider something else: Your doubts and self-judgment mean you're on the right track.

We often allow this Inner Naysayer voice, Imposter Syndrome, and general internal meanness to guide us away from our leap. But what if these thoughts meant you were on the right track? What if the voice could be interpreted for what it really is—an indicator of growth and expansion—rather than mistaken as a warning of danger?

Remember, we don't want to get rid of this voice. It's more important to distinguish it from the other parts of your inner landscape so it can keep you safe when necessary and not hold you back from growth. Use these three steps to begin to identify your Inner Naysayer voice and to learn how to differentiate in the moment when it is needed and when it is getting in the way.

Imposter Syndrome

Imposter Syndrome is a persistent feeling of inadequacy despite external proof otherwise. This is the part of you that constantly fears people will learn you are a fraud, the part needing to continually prove you're worthy and then discounts all your successes, brushing them off as flukes (instead of attributing them to your abilities or hard work).

On one hand, I love Imposter Syndrome because I've found most of the highest-level visionaries possess it in some way. It's always an indicator to me that people are dreaming big, and if viewed properly can motivate and encourage people to continually apply themselves.

But on the other hand, it can be debilitating as it is marked by a persistent dialogue of unworthiness. It keeps us from truly honoring what we're creating in the world. It fails to recognize our knowledge, skills, and persistence. Studies conducted on Imposter Syndrome have shown that while they may be high-achieving, the people who suffer from this often fail to fulfill their potential (Neureiter and Traut-Mattausch 2016).

Even successful celebrities struggle with Imposter Syndrome! From Tina Fey to Emma Watson, and Maya Angelou to Kate Winslet, this is an incredibly common issue. Here are a few things to help you shift out of this behavior:

1. Begin to recognize, honor, and celebrate your accomplishments—and not just because of your charm, but because you genuinely deserve to receive the praise or rewards of your labors, which leads me to …

2. Keep track of every time you prove your value. When I began The Inspirational Woman Project, I was telling stories of hundreds of inspirational women around the globe. The issue was I didn't believe I was inspirational. After a call from a friend one afternoon, I broke down in tears with the realization I was selling something I didn't subscribe to in my own life. I committed to changing and decided to prove to myself how inspirational I was.

Every day for six months I took note of the ways I inspired the world and the people in it. I documented at least one way I was inspirational that day. Little by little my perspective began to shift, and I saw myself as inspirational. Prove to yourself you're not an imposter by continually shining light on the ways you are capable, highly skilled, and totally kickass.

3. Be of service. Shifting focus from you to others can change everything. It will get you out of your head and enable you to experience life from another perspective. Plus, it enables you to experience human connection and practice gratitude.

4. Call it out. Begin to separate yourself from the Imposter Syndrome. The more you say, "That's not me. That's Imposter Syndrome," the less of a hold it will have on you.

5. Stop comparing yourself to others. It's likely they are experiencing similar thoughts, doubts, or insecurities on the inside. Just because you can't see these things within them doesn't mean they aren't present and this person isn't struggling too. Which leads me to …

6. Take the people in your mind off the pedestals where you have put them, and remember that no one knows what they are doing.

Yeah, you heard me. No one knows what they're doing. None of us have a manual for life or business. We are all just doing the best we can every single day.

While there is a healthy level of Imposter Syndrome, it's important not to allow it to rule your life. It can paralyze you and keep you from achieving the things you desire in life.

WHY WOULD YOU EVER LEAP?

In a world doing its best night and day to push us into conformity, telling us to stay in line, it can be really easy not to leap. From very young ages, we are fed ideas we need to follow the well-worn path. Western culture tells us to stay within the confines of societal norms, focus on the rational and tangible, value traditional education, get a good-paying job, and never question anything contrary to these things.

The world around us relies on our conformity. We are inundated with all the ways we "should" be living our lives. We are taught not to trust our desires, our intuition and ourselves. We're fed fear and constantly shown all the reasons we shouldn't question our place in the world. Our educational systems are designed to turn us into mediocre worker bees, grooming our creativity and free-thinking straight out of us.

When you throw the cherry of our Inner Naysayers and Imposter Syndrome on top—with everything around us discouraging us from taking the leap—it's no wonder we perceive an "off the beaten path" venture as insane.

ALL THE EXCUSES

It's not that you don't want to commit to your vision; it's just that you may be at a point where you don't need to commit to your vision. It's not life or death. There's nothing pushing you to say "yes," which means, more often than not, your excuses for staying where you are become way more real and carry much more weight than your reasons to say "yes." Let's break down the reality of your excuses for a hot second so we can get to leaping.

1. We assume it will go wrong.

Catastrophic thinking is an experience in which people focus more on what could go wrong than what could go right. We not only assume it will go wrong, but we spin story after story of how horribly wrong it will go. This worst case scenario perspective spins us into images of homelessness, excommunication, shame, loneliness, disappointment, etc. We're conditioned to overemphasize how bad it could be if we fail. This habit of allowing theoretical future losses to dominate over theoretical future gains creates in us inaction and paralysis. In our human evolution, there was a time when this kind of thinking was necessary to survive. But remember, while our ancestors required this to stay alive, it's a practice that hinders our growth and expansion in the current human experience.

We assume a lot in life. A lot. I would venture to guess most of the stories you tell yourself in your head are assumptions and each of these assumptions tends toward the negative. No matter what you assume, your assumptions in your mind will always produce the corresponding results in your Physical World. Why not assume, possibly for the first time in your life, something will go right?

2. Self-doubt blinds us to our capacity to manage any possible consequences or risks.

We don't trust our ability to face challenges and find viable solutions. We underestimate ourselves. After we spend all this time focusing on everything that can and will go wrong, we then fail (or refuse) to see how capable we are of moving through setbacks or challenges in order to find success. We assume the challenges will break us, that we won't have the resources or support we require to succeed, and we diminish our strength, adaptability, and tenacity.

> "There is no [wo]man living who
> isn't capable of doing more than
> [s]he thinks [s]he can do."
> Henry Ford

The reality is, we learn more from taking a risk than from being comfortable. Leaping gives us the great gift of becoming aware of our potential and learning what we're capable of. We are always capable of more than we give ourselves credit for; you would surprise yourself with what you can learn, the obstacles you can conquer, and who you can become in the process. Through leaping, you will always gain more insights, experiences, success, and perspectives than you would ever be able to access if you refrained from saying "yes" to your vision.

3. We worry about what other people will think.

Thoughts of others judging and rejecting us, and our ideas, can completely rule our ability to take leaps. Our psychology is hardwired to require acceptance because, to our ancestors, lack of acceptance meant certain death. We possess an innate need to be supported by our pack in order to survive because being surrounded by the right people at the right time meant survival in the Stone Age. Today, we not only worry about what people will think if we take the first step, but also what they'll think if we fail. And, even worse yet, what if we succeed?

When you allow other people to dictate your life, you do yourself an immense disservice. Placing your life in their comfort zones will not only result in animosity for those around you, but also massive stagnation in your life. Leaping helps you push your boundaries and challenge yourself to learn because—here's the deal—we're not in the Stone Age anymore, and we don't need a community around us for basic survival. People will be threatened by your decision to change and grow, but it has nothing to do with you. Continuing to live your life for other people is not the answer. Instead, increase your self-confidence by stepping into your leap. Experience growth that could never happen if you stayed where you are, and surround yourself with people who encourage your growth and support your vision for your life.

4. We categorize failure as a bad thing.

Our brains constantly compartmentalize all the stimuli that come into our lives; right and wrong, success and failure, good and bad. It helps our computer-like minds easily distinguish experiences and input in a fast-paced world where we're all over stimulated. This prevents mental discomfort, but it can be a problem because things aren't so black and white (especially leaps, which are incredibly nuanced!). When our brain makes things black or white, it limits our outcomes.

What if failure and success could coexist? What if we could stop seeing the lack of our desired, controlled, and manipulated outcome as a bad thing? What if this outcome was exactly perfect and there was no failure?

> "A ship in harbor is safe – but that
> is not what ships are for."
> John A. Shedd

The breadth of life is experienced in the adventures and the journey. Our lives do not come with guarantees. Staying in the perceived safety of where you are does not guarantee your safety; just the same as taking this leap does not guarantee risk or failure. Leaping, however, does guarantee change, and change always presents with an equal opportunity for expansion, growth, and fulfillment. Unforeseen and unplanned greatness comes from the slight discomfort experienced during the leap process.

5. We convince ourselves mediocre isn't so bad.

Our culture is dominated with thoughts of, "If I wait long enough or behave properly or demonstrate my skills well enough, then life will just get better on its own." We make excuses and focus on mundane circumstances to explain why choosing the safe and sensible path is the smart choice. Thus, we silence and deny our potential and adhere to the status quo. We turn off the part of us that is alive and inspired and on fire, placing all our bets on a hope that "someday" it will be different.

In 2012, *The Guardian* published an article, "Top Five Regrets of the Dying," from a nurse who spent her days working with terminal patients. Her conversations with these patients revealed their top regret to be, "I wish I'd had the courage to live a life true to myself, not the life others expected of me." As it turns out, regretting not going for our desires has proven to be more harmful to our psyche than trying and failing. *Instant Guts!* author, Joan Gale Frank, says, "Even though you can come up with a dozen good excuses for why you shouldn't take a risk, there's one great big reason why you should. And that is, until you do, your heart is going to hunger. If you don't take risks, you'll never feel quite complete. Right up until the day your story ends."

6. There is too much risk associated with it.

Leaps are filled with unknown and unpredictable situations, circumstances, and events you can't control, which leads many to the conclusion it's better not to leap. If leaps have risk, then not leaping has no risk, right? Well, not exactly.

> "The biggest risk is not taking any risk."
> Mark Zuckerberg

Taking a leap does not automatically equal haphazard risk. A great amount of preparation, education, and assessment goes into the process. Rarely will you leap with your eyes closed. While we will never be able to predict everything that lies ahead, assessing all the possible outcomes is actually healthy (as long as we don't fixate and focus on the worst case scenario). Look at the array of outcomes that could come to pass, and consider the risks from all angles. There will be risks associated with leaping, but there will also be an equal amount of risk associated with not leaping.

> "We can choose to be afraid of [the future] to stand
> there trembling and not moving, assuming
> the worst that can happen or we step forward
> into the unknown and assume it will be brilliant."
> Sandra Oh

All of these reasons to leap are fabulous and totally reasonable and justified, but if I'm being honest, they all pale in comparison to the real reason to leap. The reason you picked up this book to begin with. The reason that's been whispering in your ear. The reason above all reasons.

The world needs you.

The world is craving what you possess inside—the drive and creativity only you have. It is waiting with bated breath for you to leap. No one else in this world has what you have or can do what you do with your unique perspective and your distinct voice.

Humanity will be incomplete if you don't realize your vision.

The vision you hold is like no other. Not one single human on this planet can execute it the way you can.

The world needs you.

I know sometimes it doesn't feel like it. It can feel like the world is beating you down, or a million people are executing your vision, or what you have to say isn't important, or the world will go on just fine without you.

It's not true.

Saying "yes" to your vision is the single-most important thing you could ever do. Do you believe it?

Take the time and make the effort to heal and clear your inner space so you can possess the resilience necessary to take this journey. Do whatever it takes to build your confidence and trust.

The world needs you.

In the moments you're scared, uncertain, confused, defeated, overwhelmed, tired, etc., please keep going. Give yourself momentary respite and then hear this (from my lips to your ears):

The world needs you.

I ask you now: Are you going to walk around wondering what your life could have been like? What kind of impact you could have made? What lives you could have touched if only you took a leap? Or are you going to commit to doing something about it now?

Just in case you need a reminder of how much the world needs you, visit http://permissiontoleap.today to download a note from me to you. Hang it on your bathroom mirror. Make it your phone's display screen. Keep a copy in your journal. Hide one in your wallet. Put it anywhere and everywhere to remind yourself of how much the world needs you right now.

4. The Secret to Success

THE DAILY PRACTICE

The most powerful tool I have ever encountered to support myself with the process of growth is implementing a daily inner practice. I've taken more leaps than I can count in the last fifteen years—from moving among multiple states (and countries!) to ending one business and starting another to opting out of traditional employment to closing relationships— and it wasn't until I developed my daily inner practice I was able to feel confident and secure in the leap process.

What do I mean by "daily inner practice"? It is a time when you put the Physical World on hold for a hot second. It is an everyday, dedicated time when you take the opportunity to focus all your attention into the Spiritual World. While I will go into more detail later about what this entails, it is crucial to know the purpose of the daily practice is what is most important, rather than a specific prescription of tasks.

Paying attention and adjusting your inner landscape are crucial to leaping. While everything about leaping may look like external changes to things in your Physical World, you'll learn throughout these pages that the majority of the leap is actually an inside job. It is this repetition of consciously attending to your thoughts, beliefs, and emotions that opens the space to create new habits, which then trickle into creating new ways of responding; inevitably then, new outcomes happen.

Tending to this space daily will change everything. If you continue to think the same, you will continue to act the same and feel the same, and thus create the same results. Devoting time to consistently retraining your internal state and connecting with the Spiritual World will start a ripple effect to condition your perspective little by little away from what's familiar, moving you into deeper alignment with the vision you have for your life.

Shortly before closing my fashion brand, I learned about the concept of a daily practice from Hal Elrod, author of *The Miracle Morning*. Since implementing my daily routine, I have found a resiliency and strength that have supported me and helped me take bigger leaps more regularly. I see marked improvement in my mindset; my ability to trust in the unknown and my willingness to go through the leap cycle as a result of this consistent touch point with my soul.

Let's back up briefly though because it wasn't always this way—and I don't want to mislead you into thinking this process is all sunshine and roses.

The time between the moment I decided to start my daily routine and the moment I actually did start was approximately six months. Yes, you read that correctly. I spent six months simply thinking about the idea of starting my morning practice.

Morning after morning I would lay in bed and think about doing yoga, meditating, visualizing, and setting intentions. But it took me six months to break through the barrier and actually act.

What changed that day in June? The day I finally got myself out of bed and committed to the routine that would change everything about my life?

It was a single decision amidst months and months of inner healing work. I woke up that morning and decided my future was more important than my fears. With one grand, "Fuck it!" I decided to allow my vision to lead the way, instead of allowing my present circumstances to control me. I embraced my desires and took action, even though 95 percent of my brain was screaming, "NO!"

The following day, I woke up and chose it again. And again. And again.

This is what I mean by it being a process. It's waking up day after day saying, "Yes. I choose this." That is not to say there won't be days when you decide to stay in bed. There will definitely be days you don't choose your vision. But those days become the exception to the rule instead of the ruling standard.

I also eased into implementing my daily practice. When I began implementing my morning routine, it looked nothing like it does now. In the six months I lay in bed thinking about getting up for my routine, I was convinced it had to look perfect, that if I wasn't spending an entire hour every morning touching six different activities, then it wasn't worth doing, and if I slept in by a mere three minutes, I couldn't possibly begin my practice.

But on the morning that I decided to begin, I started small and simple instead of getting overwhelmed trying to do all the things in the right order for the exact amount of time. On that morning, I committed to a simple meditation. I pulled my chair up in front of my altar and lit some sage. (Don't have an altar or sage? No problem. Remember, the most important part of this process is that you do you. Use the practices of others to guide you, but customize it to your needs.) I put on my headphones, closed my eyes, and sat in meditation for ten minutes.

That was it. That was the start of my morning routine. Ten minutes.

Little by little, day-by-day, "yes" after "yes," my routine grew into the multiple-hour experience it is now. It helped me to start small and increase my commitment. Just like boiling an egg, I slowly brought the water to a boil. It's best to gradually raise the temperature of the water and eggs together to promote even cooking and prevent cracking. If you immerse the eggs in an already boiling pot of water, they will crack.

Immerse yourself in your daily routine in a very small way and then turn the heat up. Start with one thing and commit to it day after day. Once that becomes normal, turn up the heat a little and add to your routine to ensure you don't spin yourself into a frenzy of fear and end up cracking your shell.

Gay Hendricks describes this beautifully in *The Big Leap*. He explains how each of us has an inner thermostat set to our own personal "normal."

Say, for example, your normal is 75°F. You're going along living your life at 75°F—all your habits, experiences, relationships, etc. are set at this temperature.

But one day something happens: you decide to leap, or you win the lottery or meet your soul mate or get offered your dream job. Your thermostat jumps instantaneously to 100°F, far surpassing your comfort zone of 75°F. Throwing yourself that far out of your comfort zone is probably going to crack your shell, which will be followed very quickly by your body and mind doing anything and everything to bring you back to your normal.

You'll back away from your leap, spin into bankruptcy, sabotage your relationships, or get fired ... simply to return to 75°F ... when instead, you could have eased into the experience and turned your heat up gradually so as to avoid the backlash. This book is filled with activities and exercises to help you turn your temperature up gradually, starting with your daily practice.

THREE KEYS TO BUILDING YOUR PRACTICE

1. Determine your own combination of activities that work for you. Start with experimenting to determine what supports you and makes you feel great and what leaves you feeling worse. You'll need to work through the discomfort of newness to figure out what actually works because alignment may not happen instantaneously. Give it some time. Commit to trying something for ten days and then reassess.

Activities that could work for you include meditation, yoga, breath work, Solfeggio tones, taking a walk, reading, journaling, coloring, eating a healthy breakfast, going to the gym, sitting on your patio in silence, visualization, dance parties, affirmations, gratitude, intention-setting, etc. Tools are scattered throughout this book to be used during your daily practice as well.

2. Allow it to be fluid. In my daily practice, no two days ever look the same. When I wake up in the morning, I ask myself, "What do I need

today?" Some days it might be meditation, visualization, yoga, and breath work. Other days may be coloring mantras while listening to Solfeggio tones. And other days may simply be lying on the living room floor with the kitties in deep gratitude for an hour. Give yourself permission to honor your needs in the moment every day.

3. Feel into what works best for you. A lot of daily practice guidelines push the idea that this must be a morning practice. It doesn't have to be. Maybe it's a break at lunch, or an evening ritual before you go to sleep, or a combination of two different times during the day. I personally prefer the morning time to connect with my soul. I feel it nourishing to start each day with the energy of possibility and allow that to be the road map for the remainder of my day. But this doesn't work for everyone. You may prefer to do it before bed to close your day so that you wake up and can immediately start your day.

Boiling down these three points into the essence of what's important looks like this: While other people may have recommendations for how best to implement this, your daily practice is yours and yours alone. It's imperative you take the time and apply the energy to determine what works best for you. Yes, listen to what experts have to say, but at the end of the day, it's up to you to take what works and leave the rest.

MAKE IT YOUR OWN

What you *do* during your practice doesn't matter. The purpose is what this practice creates for you: space and connection.

1. Space

We live in a world where being busy is glamorous, where we fill every waking hour with a distraction, an app, a meeting, a conversation, a podcast, or an appointment. We run from one thing to another, and when we find ourselves in a place of stillness, we just whip out our phones to distract us again. We're inundated with stimuli we can't even wait in line at the grocery store for five minutes without needing to fill that time with something.

Does this "fullness" affect your leap? Yes, because if your life is full, there will be no space for something new to come in.

Imagine a closet. This closet is full—literally bursting at the seams. You can barely close the door, and when you do, you're afraid to open it because all the contents will spill out everywhere. The hangers are jam-packed together, and every single one is used. In addition to the hangers, you have clothes thrown over the closet rod and folded in piles on the floor.

What happens when you want to buy something new? You don't have space for what's currently in there, much less any additional items. Adding to your wardrobe is not an option.

This work is similar. If every waking moment of your life is filled, there is no space to realize your dreams. There is no opportunity for the Universe to speak to you or provide clarity because your mind is always full. Your vision cannot grow (or even be born) because it doesn't have space to exist.

Your daily practice provides this time free from distractions giving you the space needed for your vision to breathe.

2. Soul Connection

Your daily practice should strengthen the relationship you have with yourself, as well as the Spiritual World, and bring about the growth of your soul. I like to think of it as a relationship with a new person. When you are dating someone new or have a new friendship in your life, how do you create a strong, lasting connection? You spend time together and consistently connect to strengthen the bond between the two of you. It's Relationship Building 101.

The same is true when it comes to building a new pathway for your life. Consistently connecting with your heart, your soul, and your vision every day will strengthen the bond you have with yourself and with the unseen, and in turn, will create a new way of relating to yourself and the world around you.

You wouldn't turn to a new friend or significant other and say, "I want all the benefits of having you in my life, but I want to put in zero effort," or, "I want the best relationship with you, but I don't ever want to talk. I don't actually care about getting to know you." No, you would show up and connect with that person. Be it a short text exchange, a conversation over a meal, or a multiple-hour phone conversation, you would show up, connect, and build a relationship with that person. This is an opportunity for you to give yourself the same gift.

3. Consistency

Consistency is one of the most important factors in improving the probability for the successful outcome you desire. It breeds trust, increases your communication with your intuition, strengthens your confidence in the process, provides clarity in the next steps, bolsters an inner stability to support you in taking action, and creates the results you desire more quickly.

We've all had the friend who only calls us when shit is going wrong or when they need something, right? How does it feel to be on the receiving end of that? It generally feels terrible, as if this person is abusing your friendship and using your kindness only for their gain. We all desire to be seen, heard, and supported in relationships, and the relationship between yourself and the Spiritual World is no different. If you're only calling on it when you need it, it's going to stop picking up your calls.

So, yes, it's important to call on this energy when you are in need. But it's even more important to connect with it in the times you don't need it. The consistency in that connection will change everything for you and create an inner resiliency that will bring more ease and peace into the leap process.

Throughout the rest of this book are more thorough examples as to specific exercises you can incorporate into your daily practice time, including visualization, meditation, gratitude, rituals, and mantras to help get you started.

CREATE NEW HABITS

When you are starting something new, there will always be resistance. I'm talking about the kind of resistance where your heart desperately wants the change and the leap you seek, but you just can't seem to get the momentum behind you to take the actions; the kind of resistance where your conscious mind says "yes," but everything about your subconscious screams "no."

This book will begin to disrupt and muddy the waters of your current habits, understandings, and perspectives. It is up to you to create new habits to align with your desires. Holding onto old, habitual ways of being will not support your leap.

Dr. Joe Dispenza explains habits as a state of being "when your body is your mind. A habit is an unconscious set of thoughts behaviors and emotions that are acquired through frequent repetition." What he means is that habits happen so your body can continue on auto-pilot without your brain needing to consciously engage.

Through conscious repetition, your brain detects a pattern and stores the information into your subconscious. It's a process that conditions your body to override your mind.

Have you ever picked up your phone to dial a number and a few minutes later find yourself scrolling through your Instagram feed? Or you open your laptop to search for something, and you go on auto-pilot, coming back to consciousness 20 minutes later to find you've been taken down the rabbit hole of Facebook or YouTube? Or you get out of the shower with no recollection of the experience? Or you look back on your drive home and have no memory of it?

You have performed those activities so many times your conscious brain doesn't need to be present because your body remembers it.

Dr. Dispenza notes "this is the problem because once the body knows better than the mind, then 95% of who we are is the body-mind. When it comes time to change you use 5% of your conscious mind going against 95% of what you've memorized subconsciously, this is where the trouble happens. Because you can think positively all you want, but if you've been feeling negatively for 35 years, that's mind and body in opposition. You can create your dream board with all your beautiful pictures of your dream house and your SUV and everything else, but then you could feel unworthy because mind and body are in opposition. The challenge is that we have to recondition the body and the mind, and that's the work to do to work in order to change patterns." (Larré, 2014)

When I considered incorporating this daily practice into my life, I knew deep down the truth of this activity wasn't as simple as taking a few actions every day. I was incredibly aware that beginning this morning routine, everything about my life would change.

This is the exact reason it took me six months to implement my daily practice. My conscious mind was 110 percent in for the change, but as Dr. Dispenza explains, that accounts for only 5 percent of the decision-making process. And unfortunately, the other 95 percent of my brain was not on board with undergoing the massive change and transformation—or at least it wasn't on board until I made the commitment to recondition my mind to change the pattern. I made a conscious decision to wake up every day and choose my future over and over again.

Are there days when I choose not to do my morning routine? Days when staying in bed with the kitties takes priority? Days when I'm on vacation and deserve to sleep in a bit? Yes, absolutely. No one is perfect.

In those moments, I invite you to remember to be easy on yourself. Feeling bad about your decision will neither change your mind nor make you want to say "yes" tomorrow. Take a day to chill out and allow yourself to pause. Then wake up tomorrow and recommit to saying "yes" to your vision.

Remember: Leaps may begin with a one-time decision, but they are so much more than that. Leaps are a series of small yeses strung together day after day. Leaps are about taking one bite, one step, one day at a time.

Part Two:

THE SIX PHASES OF A LEAP

5. The Fence of Indecision

I returned to the United States in 2006, fresh off of two years in Italy studying fashion. After a temporary summer job as a costume designer, which paid me pennies, I knew I would need to either move home or figure out another source of income.

Within a week of searching for work in my new city, Olympia, Washington, I had not only scored myself a free living arrangement in exchange for getting two small children off to school every morning, but I also landed a position as a receptionist.

I was set. With very minimal expenses, I found my savings account growing with each passing week, and I even decided to start a little fashion company in my spare time to satisfy my soul. I had no visions of grandeur with the business. Heck, I didn't even want to be an entrepreneur. But I knew if I wasn't tapping into my passion on a regular basis, my existence would become very bleak very quickly.

Week by week my day job started trusting me more. In addition to answering phones and filing, they began to assign me case-file reviews. Then I was asked to develop job analyses. Then I was asked to conduct labor market research.

Around month three, my bosses offered me a raise and promotion. I would need to help find my replacement for the receptionist position, but I was doing such a great job, they wanted me to become a vocational rehabilitation counselor intern.

I barely considered the offer before I declined it. Not only was I happy where I was, after observing my coworkers, I knew in my heart the job was not for me.

A month later, I was pulled into another meeting with my bosses. They were so impressed with my task completion rate, they wanted me to reconsider the offer they had made. I was resolute in my decision—that job was not for me.

Then life began to wear me down. As it turned out, making ten dollars an hour wasn't as glamorous as I had anticipated. I got the itch to move, but I couldn't afford rent. My heart yearned to travel again, but airfare was expensive. My car started acting up, and while I wanted a new one, I couldn't take on a car payment. Yes, I'd been saving up with minimal expenses, but if I started living beyond my means with rent and travel and a car payment ... my savings wouldn't last very long.

A few weeks later my bosses approached me again with an offer to reconsider. I knew that if I wanted to live the life I desired, I needed to earn more money. In consideration of the doubled income, I accepted the promotion and instantaneously felt the click of golden handcuffs that would remain locked around my wrists for seven years. This is what everyone did though, so I'd just have to deal with it.

It wasn't so bad at first. I moved in with a roommate and was enjoying the considerably larger income. I found the ability (or maybe naïveté) to distract myself enough so I didn't focus on how out of integrity this job was for me. My little fashion company was still a hobby. I was enjoying the periodic commission for a prom or flower girl dress, and I wasn't mentally in the space to see myself as an entrepreneur.

The problem was the pain of being out of integrity would creep in periodically, and I would find myself devastated by having to turn off my heart and deny my passion every day. My thoughts about work always journeyed along this path: *It's not what I want, but it's here right now. It's my reality. It's paying the bills. I can't say "no" to that, can I? I'd better just stay at this job until something better presents itself. I can deal with the discomfort and lack of fulfillment. I'm fine.*

And I was fine—or pretended I was for a few months before the same loop of thoughts crept in again. More and more often, I found myself at this crossroads going back and forth between staying and going, money and soul, survival and fulfillment.

For seven years I remained uncommitted to staying and uncommitted to leaving. For seven years I went back and forth between, "I hate it and need out," and, "It's not so bad. I'll stay for the money."

While the first year wasn't so bad, each passing year got worse and worse. Plus the growth of my fashion business and my entrepreneurial spirit kicking into overdrive didn't help the situation any. Little by little, my awareness of my purpose, vision, and possibility grew. I went from making the periodic special-occasion dress to headlining shows in Seattle, gracing magazine covers, and winning awards for my designs.

I slipped into a reclusive, depressed, barely functioning state on multiple occasions. Toward the end of year five, I rarely left my house. I turned my third bedroom into my office and fallen into a trap of rolling out of bed into the office, working for several hours, feeding myself, returning to work for several more hours, and then spending the evenings on my couch. Showering became a special-occasion activity. Most days I didn't even pull my curtains; it was rainy and gray outside anyway, so what did it matter?

In addition to the lack of fulfillment ripping my heart to shreds, the indecision was exhausting. It took everything I had just to make this rotation in my small home, much less having to leave, interact with humans, and take care of my basic needs.

But this wasn't me. My behavior was a deep indication I was completely out of alignment with my heart and soul, but I was not able to trust the Spiritual World enough to surrender into my entrepreneurial vision. I didn't feel safe believing in the possibility of what I was creating and instead relied totally on seeing. I put my power in the hands of others (namely my bosses) and failed to commit to or create this craving that had been simmering under the surface for years—all while I fooled myself into believing running my business on the side was enough for me.

All the stimuli running my decisions were based in the Physical World because that's what was "supposed" to be making my decisions. I focused on the steady paycheck and the rational reasons I needed to keep my job. And every time I got remotely close to the edge of quitting, I'd be tempted back into the logic with a job offer, promotion, decrease in my hours, or increase in my flexibility.

Around my seven-year anniversary, things went from bad to incredibly worse. Thankfully, I had relocated to Los Angeles during this time and was able to telecommute, which had eased my depressive state for a hot second. But then the anxiety kicked in.

I couldn't even look at my work laptop without an increase in my heart rate, racing thoughts, and sweaty palms.

I was nearing my breaking point, but I still couldn't bring myself to leave. On one hand, I was begging for the job to go away, and on the other, I was hanging on so tightly nothing could shake the death grip I had on it. I was being pulled in opposite directions with every breath.

It left me in bed a lot—more than I'd like to admit—and I even voiced to my mom that if this job was the rest of my life, I'd rather die.

How was it I was allowing myself to exist in a voluntary misery that I most definitely could have changed if I'd wanted? How was it I could be so out of alignment and in pain, and yet so unwilling to do anything about it?

INDECISION WILL GET YOU NOWHERE

The first phase in any leap process is to get off the fence. What fence is this, you may ask? The Fence of Indecision. On one side is your leap, on the other side is not your leap. And you're right in the middle with a fence up … well, you get the picture.

I'm guessing you've probably been hanging out on this fence for a while, looking to the left at your leap and to the right at your not leap. Left or right. Leap or not. You can tell how long you've been on this fence based on the amount of pain you're currently experiencing. I mean, sitting on a fence isn't easy (talk about a core workout!), nor is it comfortable. And don't even get me started on the splinters.

Indecision is easily one of the biggest killers of visions. Not only does it result in stagnation, exhaustion (it drains physical and emotional energy), anxiety, and lack of confidence, but it also prevents you from moving forward in any direction whatsoever—which is exactly where I found myself.

I couldn't move forward in my job, nor could I move forward out of my job because I refused to commit to either option. I was energetically drained. I had invested so much thought, so many emotions, and so much fear into this decision—rather this indecision—I had nothing left to give. My fight-or-flight response was pretty much on high alert constantly, causing massive adrenal issues and placing my physical body under ridiculous amounts of stress. I didn't trust myself, and I didn't know where to turn.

This confusion of energy and waffling back and forth between the two sides of the fence can keep you in limbo indefinitely. Only a definitive commitment to one direction will enable you to move forward.

The popular book Think and Grow Rich cited indecision as the thirteenth (out of thirty) most common cause of failure.

"Slowness in making decisions or the inability
to make decisions will tie
one to the treadmill of failure."
Napoleon Hill

Decide what it is you want. Committing to saying "yes" or "no" to your vision, your desires, your truth begins to reveal a path for you where there was none before.

Decisiveness opens doors. It doesn't matter what side of the fence you choose. The Spiritual World does not differentiate between good and bad or right and wrong. Everything is neutral in the eyes of the Universe—that is, until we put our human expectations on it. What I mean is this: The two options you are facing are just that—options. Neither is right or wrong. They just are. It is your perspective, judgments, and expectations that turn a neutral-option molehill into a mountain of pros and cons, rights and wrongs.

The Universe simply wants us to be happy and fulfilled, and it wants to provide us with things that will satisfy us. When you fail to make a decisive choice about what you want, the Universe has no idea what to send you to create that satisfaction within you.

Imagine you're going on a trip. You decide you're leaving in early December, but you can't decide if you're going to New York or Hawaii. You go back and forth and back and forth. The Spiritual World is on pins and needles, wondering if it should send you a parka or a bikini.

This limbo causes the Spiritual World to put everything on pause because it's unclear what you want. Once you make a decision, the Spiritual World finally has guidance to know how to support you.

> "And, when you want something, all the universe
> conspires in helping you to achieve it."
> Paulo Coelho, The Alchemist

And if you don't decide, eventually the Universe will make the decision for you. We usually receive only so many hints, nudges, and winks before the Universe breaks out a massive two-by-four and knocks our ass onto one side of the fence or the other.

This is what happened to me. My refusal to decide forced the Universe to reveal its hand, and it fully kicked me to the curb. It was a kick that so much of me wanted (and I clearly needed since I wasn't getting there on my own), but it did make things increasingly more difficult.

Just after attending the California Women's Conference in 2014, I woke up from a quick nap on my couch and dreadfully forced myself to open my work laptop. I began sifting through emails and landed on one from the company's operations manager. It went a little something like this:

Just sending out a reminder that part-time employees will have their pay cut in half as of Friday.

Except Friday had happened four days ago. Wait—a reminder? Shouldn't I have gotten a first notice in order to receive a reminder? My eyes darted to the number of unread emails in my inbox, and I realized there was a good chance it was in there somewhere and I had overlooked it.

Shit. Shit. Shit.

Something similar happened to Paulo Coelho. It was August 12, 1979, and he was working as an artistic director for CBS in Brazil. At the age of thirty, he decided becoming a recording executive was much more important than his dream of being an author, and on that night as he went to bed, he made the final decision to abandon his dream. He even formulated how he would keep his love of writing pacified by composing song lyrics whenever he desired.

The Universe had other plans. Paulo Coelho woke up the following morning to a phone call from the president of his division to learn he was fired, effective immediately with no further explanation. He spent two years trying to get a job in the industry without luck. Six years later, he released his first book, and two years after that, he released *The Alchemist*, which alone has sold 35 million copies and is the most translated book in the world.

Imagine if Paulo had stuck to his decision to abandon his dream.

WHEN YOUR HEART AND HEAD ARE IN CONFLICT

Decision-making happens from two places — our head and our heart.

Decisions from the head rely more on the Physical World and use a logical approach to determine what option makes the most sense, while decisions from the heart rely more on the Spiritual World and use an intuitive approach to choose the best path.

Oftentimes, when we're in a place of indecision, it's not that we don't know what we want. It's that we're relying too much on our head and not willing to listen to the emotional, intuitive hints our body is giving us.

We've been trained to regard emotions as irrational impulses likely to lead us astray having no place in the decision-making process. So when we don't trust the possibility before us that our heart desires, our head takes over. We go into massive analysis mode and create paralysis, especially if our head and heart are in conflict.

Despite being conditioned to believe emotions get in the way of proper decision-making, it has been proven that emotions are crucial to the process.

Over a thirty-year period, neuroscientist Antonio Damasio from the University of California, Los Angeles, studied people with damage to the area of the brain where emotions are generated. These were people who presented as "normal," except they were unable to feel emotions. The common thread between each of his subjects became very apparent: they couldn't make decisions.

His findings were published in a 1994 book entitled *Descartes' Error: Emotion, Reason and the Human Brain*. He discovered the subjects could describe the decision logically, but they had significant difficulty moving past the list of pros and cons to actually commit to things as simple as what to eat.

Damasio concluded emotions are an incredibly important—nay, crucial—factor for decision-making. His study showed that even when we believe our decisions are based on rational facts, the final pinnacle of choice always boils down to an emotional motivation.

"An important aspect of the rationalist conception is in order to obtain the best results, emotions must be kept out," Damasio observed, "[that] rational processing must be unencumbered by passion."

While this view is generally regarded as truth, Damasio proved this belief does not remain true when you begin to dive into the biological mechanics of decision-making. The results for the brain-trauma victims in the cases and histories Damasio studied were clear: the physical damage caused to the brains resulted in a significant decrease in their ability to experience emotion, which, in turn, profoundly diminished their capacity to reason and make decisions. In short: the less emotion we feel, the lower our decision-making ability is.

Damasio concluded, "Reduction in emotion may constitute an equally important source of irrational behavior," and to make the correct call, one needs to feel their way to the conclusion.

As you may remember, your leap will never "make sense" in your rational mind. Your feelings, emotions, and intuition are going to be the key to guiding you through your leap.

YOUR INTUITION IS GOLD

The correlation between intuition and decision-making was also studied by Joel Pearson, an associate professor of psychology at the University of New South Wales in Australia. As the lead author of the study, Pearson worked with his colleagues performing experiments to determine whether or not people were using their intuition to help guide their decision-making.

The results were published online in *Psychological Science* in April 2016 (Lufityanto, Donkin, and Pearson) and indicated that people who used their intuition in decision-making were able to come to faster and more accurate conclusions in a more confident manner. This method accesses our subconscious and oftentimes does not make rational sense. Intuitive decisions cannot be addressed with reason, but instead materialize quickly out of instinct—we know the right answer long before our logical brain catches up.

Their secondary conclusion was the participants also became better at using their intuition over time. "It's all about learning to use unconscious information in your brain," he said. People become accustomed to making decisions when they use logic, but they also strengthen their intuitive muscles when they use them more frequently over time.

Why then, if we know our logical reasoning is preventing us from making the best decisions, do we continue to rely on it as our top resource for decision-making?

Logical reasoning is ripe for paralysis by over analysis. It allows our brain to nitpick every single option and every single outcome. It encourages us to gather more and more information—most of which our brain cannot process because it's already too full and overwhelmed. Worst of all, logical reasoning keeps us distracted from feeling and hearing our intuition.

If you were to truly allow yourself the space to access your feelings when making decisions, it would save you time, mental anguish, and loads of stress. Yes, it can feel so important to identify the risks and rewards of your decision to leap, but at the end of the day, your heart and intuition are the best guiding lights when it comes to getting off the fence.

I know what you're going to say: "But what if I make the wrong decision?"

Setting aside the fact I don't believe in right or wrong, I want to remind you it's better to make a "wrong" decision and course correct than to make no decision at all. Why? A "wrong" decision will begin to give you feedback about whether to keep moving forward with your commitment, or to refocus your attention on a different trajectory.

Our intuition always knows the answers. We're just unwilling to really listen and trust.

Had I trusted my inner voice and the clues and hints all around me, I could have saved myself the painful experience of my pay being abruptly cut in half. Using my intuition would have given me an immediate answer; instead, my brain took seven years to reason in and out of the decision. I knew the entire time I needed to leave my job, but I held on so tightly the Universe had no option but to make the decision for me.

ASKING FOR ADVICE IS A TERRIBLE IDEA

When faced with a decision and logic kicks in, our brain decides it's a great idea to go ask everyone we know what they would do in the same situation.

> "Advice is what we ask for when we already
> know the answer but wish we didn't."
> Erica Jong

Here's the deal: asking for advice is a terrible idea—not because your friends and family possess bad judgment, but rather people will always give you answers based on their perspective.

Say you want to start a business, so you reach out to your closest friend. This friend has known you for years, supports you like crazy, and wants nothing but the best for you. The issue is this friend is not business-minded. They work a steady nine-to-five corporate job and plan to retire from the same position in thirty years.

Why is this an issue? Their perspective doesn't align with yours. They will likely discourage you from starting the business and encourage you to stay with the route perceived to be more stable because of their point of view and where their values are aligned. They're going to give you the "truth" based on their perception.

It's as if they're viewing the world through red lenses and you're viewing it through blue lenses. So when they look at the sky, their truth is purple while your truth is blue. The aligned decision for someone who is an entrepreneur is going to be drastically different from the aligned decision for someone who is comfortable as a corporate employee—which is perfectly fine (and normal!).

Simply be aware that going to someone who hasn't experienced the results you want will not guide you in the right direction. If you choose to receive input from someone, be very discriminatory about whom you seek out. Find a mentor, coach, or advisor currently experiencing the results you desire and ask them questions about their experience.

But remember, even if this person has experienced the results you desire, no one can fully know your viewpoint or your trajectory but you because it exists only within you. Asking someone else to make your decision for you causes their life trajectory to become yours. It doesn't work. Your path is unique to you. Use your intuition as your North Star. Let it guide you. Trust that even if you have no proof in the Physical World, the Spiritual World will take care of you.

If you can't yet get to a place where you fully trust yourself to make decisions from an emotional place, start small and strengthen your intuitive reasoning skills with decisions that don't have such do-or-die consequences. You may recall from Chapter 2, starting to use your intuition for things that don't involve emotions is the best way to start. The following are some ways you can begin to play with your intuition:

- Allow your intuition to show you which route to drive home.

- Let it guide you to which avocados to purchase at the grocery store.

- Have it lead you to the cafe, restaurant, or bar you should go for dinner.

- Use it to reveal the activities of your daily practice.

TO LEAP OR NOT TO LEAP

Now, obviously this book is about taking leaps in life, but I want to point out that if you decide not to leap, the choice is completely available to you. As I mentioned before, I don't believe in right or wrong. If you decide to stay where you are now, it's your choice. Just don't be fooled into thinking there won't be consequences if you ignore your heart.

This would be a great time to revisit your intention(s) for this book. Are you going to stand on the sidelines like a Spectator, simply watching from afar, or are you going to immerse yourself, say "yes" to your vision, and be the Creator that you know you are?

While there are risks, rewards, and consequences to leaping, there is an equal number of risks, rewards, and consequences to NOT leaping. It's just a matter of determining which risks, rewards, and consequences hold more weight for you and adjusting your commitment accordingly.

For as many leaps as I've taken, there is a long list of leaps I said "no" to as well. In college, I pulled my application to attend the Fashion Institute of Technology (FIT). After a friend was rejected, I became terrified I wasn't good enough and didn't want to face the same rejection. I think I experienced more anxiety and discomfort with her rejection than she did.

I was been planning to attend Fashion Institute of Technology (FIT) for three years. In fact, it was the sole reason I attended college in North Dakota. I could stay in my comfort zone by attending school in North Dakota, and take advantage of their cooperative exchange program with FIT to move to New York at some far off time in the future. But when it became real, my fears took center stage: If (more like when) FIT rejected me, there was no way I believed I would emotionally recover from it. Instead of allowing myself to be vulnerable to risk, I stopped my application process.

And while I felt great, not receiving the rejection letter, it meant passing on my deep, decade-long desire to live in New York City. It meant I had just wasted three years in North Dakota, when I could have attended college anywhere in the country. It meant severe disappointment in myself because I gave up on what I desired more than anything. It meant I got to looked in the mirror every day to see a girl who was controlled more by her fears than her dreams.

Regardless of what you decide, you will gain things and you will sacrifice things. What's most important to you? What are you willing to risk for your dreams? If you look forward to your later years, will you regret not trying?

So there you sit on the fence. On one side is your leap. On the other side is not your leap. And, like I mentioned before, you're sitting right in the middle with a fence up … well, you get the picture.

To leap or not to leap, that is the question.

What will it be?

Before you make your decision, give yourself some space to be present with what's happening inside you. Lean on the tools you use on a daily basis to guide and support you in this decision—this is why you practice in the first place. Use your daily practice to connect to the Spiritual World and get curious.

Incorporating curiosity into your decision-making process will enable you to approach the situation from a place of open energy and to explore the possibilities, versus approaching the situation from a closed energy, blocking the possibilities from being presented to you.

Evan Polman, PhD, conducted a study at the University of Wisconsin-Madison regarding decision-making and curiosity (Polman, Ruttan, and Peck 2016). He and his colleagues performed four experiments revealing how curiosity-based inquiries can help people steer toward more positive actions. You can rely on curiosity to support yourself in making smarter, healthier decisions, as well as to lower the stress and tension associated with the decision.

Buddha was known for saying the root of all suffering is attachment. I like to add "and unmet expectations." Perpetuating your stress spiral, holding onto and attaching to your desired expectations, and rationalizing what makes sense will only lead you astray. Instead, use the exercises outlined here and access my worksheet to guide your decision-making process. You will find that tapping into the unseen, approaching the situation from curiosity, and getting still will be immensely supportive in providing clarity regarding what you truly desire, enabling you to get off the fence of indecision to commit to your leap (or not).

Worksheet:

1. My heart wants me to:
2. But my fears are: (address thoughts and feelings)
3. How does it feel to choose my wants?

4. What emotions arise when I think about saying "yes" to my desire?

5. How does it feel to choose my fears?

6. What emotions arise when I think about saying "no" to my desire?

7. What are my core values in life?

8. Am I willing to trust my emotions and feelings to guide my decision?

9. Am I committed to my leap? Why or why not?

You realize your best progress through action, not consumption (am I right, Creator?). To do this exercise properly, access my official worksheet, which includes ample space to write your answers. Simply go to http://permissiontoleap.today to download this free resource.

6. Align with Your Vision

Shortly before this book began to call to me, I took a trip to Bali and made a commitment to my life and business that scared the shit out of me. I had no idea at the time, but I was committing to the biggest leap of my life to date.

Let's back up a second though. Why Bali? No, it wasn't because of Eat, Pray, Love. During one of my many vision-board creations approximately ten years earlier, I came across a six-page spread for a retreat center in Ubud. It called to me so intensely that I have transferred this same magazine spread to every vision board I have created in the last decade.

For ten years I waited for the "right" time. I looked at the worn, faded magazine spread for a decade. Year after year, I allowed the rationalizations of the Physical World to keep me from a trip my heart yearned for.

Fast-forward to July 2016. Having closed my fashion brand fifteen months earlier, I wrapped the largest month of my coaching business, training thousands of women in creating and manifesting the life they deserve and desire. Hell, it wasn't just the largest month of my coaching business— it was the largest month of my entrepreneurial career. And by "largest month," I mean I brought in double my previous year's income in a single month. I was insanely proud of what I achieved and so inspired by the incredible number of women I trained in such a short period of time.

A sense of complete satisfaction in my heart mixed with utter exhaustion in every other part of my body. My soul was on fire, but my physical body was having a hard time keeping up. I applied a ridiculous amount of energy to create my success. I had no idea what I was committing to when I agreed to train over 2,000 women at one time.

It was the Fourth of July, and I lay in bed listening to the fireworks outside, watching Netflix. I began to daydream about getting out of Los Angeles for some much-needed rest and healing. After pausing my movie, I conducted a simple Google search for cheap international flights.

One click led to another click, which led to another search, which led to some more clicks, and at the end of it all, I had a ticket to Denpasar in my inbox. I was finally answering the call of my soul. I marked my calendar for the flight that would land me in Bali in five months for a much-needed escape, then I turned my movie back on to relax with a huge smile on my face, knowing what was to come.

As time inched closer to my trip, I heard story upon story of friends who traveled to Bali, all of which included the magic and serendipity of the island. In the spirit of having a relaxing trip, I decided I would not plan anything until I arrived (aside from my lodging and airport transportation, of course—a girl needs to have a little bit of a plan, am I right?). I surrendered into the flow and freedom of my adventure and let go of any expectations about how it would all play out.

On my first morning waking up at Roam Co-Living to the sounds of roosters and geckos, I lay in bed to finally sift through all the recommendations sent my way. From hikes, to restaurants, to monkeys, to healers, I started to see my trip unfold little by little. I booked myself a day at the spa and would take the Camphau Ridge walk to get there. I was committed to trying every single thing on the menu at Alchemy. I reserved my place in a sound healing at the Yoga Barn. I found the best street for shopping.

The one area that I was particularly focused on during my stay was visiting healers. Not only was I slowly healing from a medical issue I've battled for years, I was committing to developing a deeper sense of peace about my long-term financial situation, shedding some of my past beliefs around entrepreneurialism, and stepping into a bigger version of myself, especially after powerfully creating my business revenue that year. Experiencing my largest year in business in the decade of being an entrepreneur, I worried my successes could have been a fluke, but I was unwilling to go backwards from that point.

While researching healers, I found a review of a healer in Ubud that sounded like the perfect fit, but I wasn't quite ready. It can be tricky, using only the Internet, to know which healers are legit, so I messaged a girlfriend who had recently visited and asked for a referral.

Her short-and-sweet response came an hour later: Devi Ma.

Why did the name sound so familiar? I scrolled back through all my open tabs and there it was. The review I found was for the same woman. There are no coincidences. I immediately opened a new browser and pulled up my email. A week later, I was walking up to her villa, past the koi pond, and into her healing studio.

We began by talking about why I had come to Bali, how I found her, and what I was seeking from our time together. Within a matter of minutes, she discovered on a major area of resistance in me.

"What are you waiting for?" she asked.

"I don't wait for anything in life. Ever," I scoffed.

Without hesitation, she calmly responded, "Well, then why can't you build a million-dollar business now? You don't need to build or grow incrementally. You can aim for it now."

I was stunned. Was that even possible?

This lighthearted, passing invitation would change my life. I spent the next week playing with the possibility of what a million-dollar business could look like for my clients, the women of the world, and me. And by the time I returned to the States, I was semi-committed to this expansion.

Now, I will admit it took me another month to fully commit to it. I sat on that fence leaning left and right: Did I want it or not? Was it important to me or not? Little by little, possibilities opened up all around me. I began to see the opportunities I could create for other women in the world by saying "yes" to this vision. And I received message after message during my meditations encouraging me to commit until I finally had no other option.

The moment I decided I was 100 percent in for this new trajectory, everything in my life began to fall apart. Everything that worked in my business the year prior simply stopped working. Where I would have hundreds of active women in my online training challenge, I saw only a handful of actively engaged women. Where I easily filled my group training programs in the year prior, I saw only a third of the enrollment this time around.

I built a life and a business fully aligned with my old six-figure trajectory of success and planned out my upcoming year to fit my former vision. For the last decade of being an entrepreneur, my trajectory focused on survival, and Devi's invitation to build a million-dollar business changed everything. I was playing small. I believed there were incremental steps to building an empire. I believed it had to take time and I wasn't ready yet.

My vision of what was possible expanded at a rapid rate, and all the sudden, nothing I planned for 2017's business was working. The things in my Physical World were not in support of my new direction and my expanded vision could not simultaneously coexist with it.

Day after day, I lost my momentum. I felt as if I was walking through a fog. No new inspiration or direction was coming to me. I was grasping at straws, wishing and hoping and praying something would take.

I felt like the Universe had abandoned me. After revealing this massive possibility and vision to me, it encouraged me to commit … and disappeared. I would get partial insights, and then nothing again.

In a meditation in January, I clearly heard, "You're writing a book this year. And you're leaving Los Angeles in June for two weeks to write it." I asked over and over again for more information: What am I writing about? Where am I going? How can I book travel if I don't have any information? Nothing.

My discomfort and frustration grew and grew and grew. I had no inspiration to show up for my business or myself. I spent weeks on end binge-watching *Mr. Selfridge, The Good Wife,* and *Suits.* I felt guilty because I should be doing something. I kept shaming myself because I was supposed to be building this million-dollar business, and yet there I was, dawdling about with no direction or inspiration, as day after day, more things were stripped from my life.

Over the course of just a few months, multiple friendships dissolved. I became acutely aware I would need to end a second business I had been managing for two years, including the associated podcast. The systems I set up to support myself all fell away. It felt like everything I built in the previous year was for naught.

I totally fell into the trap of defining my reality by what I could see in my life. I allowed myself to feel like shit as I disconnected from the Spiritual World and fell deeper into the Physical World. It took over my thoughts, attitude, and beliefs. All I could think about was how I was failing in my business, in my relationships, and in the goal I had committed myself to.

It sucked. I was angry and so frustrated. Why was everything falling apart? I made the commitment and received the inspiration to move forward on this path, but so far it was terrible. Why would the Spiritual World open up such an opportunity for me and then leave me without the things I needed to make it my reality?

I was totally playing the victim and, in doing so, failed to see the Universe providing me glimpses day after day. Little by little, the energy was opening up.

I received a text in February from some friends:
Hey there! We are going to Europe at the end of June. Any chance you want to housesit for us in Seattle? We have three cats that would make good writing muses. We'll be gone for two weeks.

Two weeks. In June. Out of Los Angeles. To write. After weeks and weeks of worrying about how the message from my meditation was going to play out in the Physical World, the Spiritual World was taking care of it all along. But because I couldn't see it, I didn't trust it was happening.

Not only was the message I received in January spot-on, it was better than I could have imagined. Turns out, I'd have a four-story townhouse to myself, with three kitties, a car, and a free flight. My needs would be completely taken care of without the hassle of hotels, I would be able to cook without having to rely on restaurants, and I wouldn't need to worry about getting a rental car.

Shortly after my tickets were purchased for my writer's retreat in Seattle, the contents for my book began to trickle into my existence. I had an epiphany about my zone of genius. A light bulb went off, revealing my ten-week program was not doing what I intended or creating the long-lasting results I wanted for my clients. The entire structure for the *Permission to Leap* brand came into view. I hired a marketing team.

And right around the time this was all happening, it hit me. I had been looking at it all wrong. I know this shit (and clearly teach it), yet the trap of the Physical World is so seductive. It lured me into its lair and caused me to lose my connection with the Spiritual World.

The week of June fifth I was reading my horoscope as I always do, but this week, Chiani Nicholas' words hit me like a lightning bolt: "In order to master our energy and our sense of self-worth, we must be able to honor the departures as much as we do the arrivals."

As often as I teach all of these concepts, when you're in the thick of it, sometimes it's hard to remember them for yourself. I forgot that in order for something new to come into my life, there must be space for it to exist.

From my perspective, everything was going wrong and falling apart, when, in fact, everything was going perfectly right and falling apart.

My life wasn't falling apart because it was wrong; it was falling apart to make space for what I was building. After all, you can't build a new vision on an old, cracked, and crumbling foundation.

The perspective I was living by all year was that the destruction and turmoil in my life were misplaced. I was hanging on to what had been, believing it would all come with me into my new vision. The problem was the things in my life were aligned with my former vision and were no longer in alignment with the shift in my vision.

It's always chaotic in the middle of anything because it's impossible to create something new without making a bit of a mess. If you're baking a cake, the kitchen is going to look like a disaster. If you're in the middle of a surgery, the operating room and doctors are going to be covered in blood. If you're doing a puzzle, the table is going to be covered in pieces. If you're making art, you will be covered in paint or clay.

Things must fall apart in order to be put back together in a new configuration. Creation cannot happen without some destruction.

IT'S AN ALIGNMENT ISSUE

Once you have gotten off the fence and made your decision to leap, the Universe will reveal all the areas and things in your life that don't fit with this new commitment. Relationships, businesses, living situations, interactions and conversations, events and experiences will begin to feel off and unfulfilling. Things in your life now resonate with your current experience, but they don't necessarily resonate with the direction you're growing toward.

Looking at it from the outside and seeing all of these things fall away could very easily lead you to believe you made the wrong decision. I mean, your entire world is collapsing (or at least portions of it are!). This means you should abandon your leap and go back to safety, right? Wrong.

This is the stage where people experience the most confusion. You make the commitment. You get excited and think this is it—the leap is coming. Then, life as you know it begins to fall apart.

Your commitment to your vision will change everything in your life. It's in this second stage that massive shifts take place in order to bring your life into alignment with your new vision. If you were just looking at the Physical World, you would likely think, "I made the wrong decision. Everything is showing me this was a terrible mistake."

But when you look at it from the added perspective of the Spiritual World, you begin to understand your life is not falling apart; it's simply misaligned. What was in alignment with your old life or goals doesn't align with your new life or goals, so things must be cleared out in order to make space for what's to come.

It's like trying to fit a square peg into a round hole. You used to have a round peg, and it fit perfectly into the round hole. But then you upgraded to a square peg. Of course it doesn't work any longer.

Or it's like having a garage that fits a Fiat, and you decide to expand your energy to the size of a Hummer. The Hummer will never fit in a garage designed for a Fiat.

In a span of six months, nearly everything I had known about my life and myself crumbled into heaps around me (with the exception of my home, which I was on the fence about releasing as well).

If I traveled down a path leading me to a six-figure business, it would look one way. And if I traveled down a path leading me to a seven-figure business, it would look completely different. The actions I take, the service I provide, the people with whom I surround myself, the beliefs I have, the way I conduct business … it all looked different.

In this stage, you must be willing to see things from a different perspective. The departure of things in your life does not mean you made the wrong decision; it means the Universe is rearranging things and making space for what you have committed to. What is taken from you is no longer necessary for your journey. Trust, let go, and release; and stop questioning why it left in the first place.

What if you completely honored the departures in your life the same way you honor the arrivals? What if we had the same "fuck yes" celebration as things leave our Physical World that we do when things enter our Physical World? What if both are equally important?

When the world seems like it's falling apart around you, remember it's not happening because you made the wrong decision. It's happening because you made the exact right decision, and it's all unfolding in perfection because you decided you want something different in your life. Instead of running the other way, what would it look like for you to declare and own your leap?

LET'S GET SCIENTIFIC FOR A HOT SECOND

Everything in the Physical World has an energetic frequency. Physicists began to research the relationship of energy and matter at the turn of the century and made significant discoveries regarding the structure and properties of atoms.

One of the biggest discoveries is that all solid matter we perceive in the Physical World is made up of 99.99999 percent space. This means that everything we experience as real in our world is only .00001 percent matter. Scientists began to recognize that everything in the Universe is made out of energy, and the things we perceive as physical in our world are not actually solid; they are mostly made up of empty space and invisible energy.

> "Everything we call real is made of
> things that cannot be regarded as real."
> Niels Bohr

Quantum physicists discovered it is the energetic frequency at which atoms vibrate that makes it solid, and it is the vibratory rate that differentiates wood from metal, or glass from a diamond. Each "thing" in our Physical World has its own unique energetic signature—including you.

> "If you want to know the secrets of the universe,
> think in terms of energy, frequency and vibration."
> Nikola Tesla

Our individual energetic vibrations affect the Physical World. When our vibrations change, they become disharmonious with certain things existing in our lives, such as relationships, businesses, jobs, living situations, etc.

The disharmony between where we are and where our vision is leading us causes these things to be eliminated from our Physical World.

In order to wrap your brain around this, let's look at it from the perspective of radio frequencies. To hear the sound associated with the station you desire, your radio has to be tuned to receive that specific energetic frequency. You don't tune into the oldies station to hear jazz. It's not what they play—it's not aligned with what their listeners expect to hear.

Now envision yourself as if you were a certain frequency on the radio dial in this moment. Maybe you're currently tuned to the country station. Imagine where on this dial the vision you are creating exists. For the sake of this example, let's say your vision is more aligned with the pop station.

In this present moment you are in alignment with exactly what your life has been. Your radio has been tuned to the country station for years. You have been accustomed to hearing the twangy music day after day. It's your normal, comfortable place in the world.

But now that you have committed to changing your vision, your radio dial needs to move. Your new vision is no longer in alignment with where your radio dial was previously tuned, and now it needs to adjust to be in alignment with this new frequency. You've been listening to country music for years, and now your tastes have changed; now you want to listen to pop music, but you'll never hear pop music if your radio is tuned to the country station.

With this new trajectory for your life and commitment to your vision, your dial is in the process of moving to the pop station. You're craving to hear solid, steady pop music coming out of your speakers, but instead you hear a jumble of static, pop, and country as the dial moves. You're in this limbo state where sometimes you're filled with confusion (static). Sometimes your new vision feels so real and present (pop). And sometimes you default back to what you've known forever (country).

But in order for your vision to be created, you have to let go of the country station. You have to continually tune your frequency to the pop station. In this phase, you need to adjust your dial ever so slightly, day after day, until all you hear is the pop station.

The more you come into alignment with your vision, the more the pop station will be the predominant sound you hear, but it's not a one-time flip of the switch. The comfort zone of your old frequency still wants to be heard, even after you commit to your new frequency.

When you change your vision, your energy begins to change, and because your energy changes, things from your old vision can't exist anymore. You cannot listen to two radio stations at the same time. The radio frequencies from country are not transmitted on the pop station—they are not in alignment.

You have previously been radiating energy of country music to the world, and now you've made the commitment to begin radiating pop music. The relationships, businesses, jobs, living situations, etc. associated and aligned with your previous radiation of energy into the world may not coexist with the new radiation of energy.

It's important to not only recognize the shift in your energetic signature vibration, but to spend time in this specific vibration. It doesn't happen overnight. You need to make conscious effort to dwell in the energy of your vision to support your radio dial in tuning to your new vision.

One of my favorite tools that supports me in existing in this new vibratory state to consciously feel and understand my new radio frequency is meditating with my future self.

Oftentimes when I ask a client what it feels like to be the future version of themselves, they have no idea. We don't know what we don't know. If we knew what it felt like to be our future self, we would already be her, am I right?

I knew there had to be a way to connect with that feeling—and not in a way that felt manufactured or forced, but in a way that illuminates and provides guidance. It's only through accessing this feeling we gain knowledge about creating it.

I remembered a quote I heard from Einstein: "For those of us who believe in physics, the distinction between past, present and future is only a stubbornly persistent illusion." What if we could tap into our future in the present moment and use the knowledge of our future to guide our present?

Leading up to a live workshop, I crafted my very first "Future-Self Meditation." The idea was the meditation would transport you into your future where you'd meet your future self, interview her, learn from her, and gain an understanding of who she is in the world. With this, you could utilize her knowledge, feelings, and insights to begin living from your future now.

On the Permission to Leap podcast, I spoke with visibility strategist Ashley Crouch about what holds us back from being our future selves. "It's said that women need to shatter the glass ceiling, which is true. However, it's important to recognize that each of us also possesses an internal glass ceiling. When we look up and see the ceiling above us, we realize it's not actually glass—it's a mirror. The reflection we see in that mirror is our own perceived self-image. Whatever that reflection is, it's as far and as high as we can achieve. We can never surpass our self-image."

The only thing standing between you and your future self is your current perception of yourself.

Why not learn about your future self and break your internal glass ceiling today? Become your future self with my "Future-Self Meditation" right now. You can access it at http://permissiontoleap.today.

BEGIN TO BRING YOUR VISION TO LIFE

People have a common misconception they need clarity and a path laid out ahead of them before talking to people about their vision. Fortunately, you don't need to know how it's going to happen or what your plan is. You don't even have to start taking action at this stage.

Unfortunately, you need to start talking about it anyway.

Taking a stand for your vision is a game changer. It's one thing to commit to your vision within yourself, but bringing others into your leap will catapult you further toward what you desire. If it remains an idea and is just hanging out in your head, it can be easy to bail on it. It's simple and safe to have an idea, a hope, a dream, but it's a completely different ball game to do something about it because it begins to make it real and hold you accountable.

The following are a few reasons why taking a stand will change everything:

1. You suddenly have skin in the game. You've incurred some sort of risk in creating your vision and now have an external push to lean on when your inner motivation wanes.

2. It reaffirms your commitment to getting off the fence. Continually repeating your dedication to your vision will drastically shift both your inner and outer alignments.

3. It's the first opportunity for your vision to make its debut in the Physical World. It's a step in moving your vision from energy into physicality.

4. It forces you to talk about your vision more often. The more you discuss it, the more your brain will begin to normalize it and build pathways to train your brain to understand this outcome as a possibility.

Failing to take a stand for your vision removes the accountability piece, meaning it could be much easier for you to back out on your commitment. Keeping your vision inside allows you to not show up for it because you can wait and hope and make excuses and hop back up on the fence. And remember what I said in the beginning: "one day" will never come. Tomorrow is a myth.

What would your Creator-self do?

In a study by psychology professor Dr. Gail Matthews (Dominican

University), successful completion of goals was increased by 33 percent when people stated their goals, shared them with friends, and implemented weekly check-ins. This was in contrast to people who merely defined their goals.

After studying 267 participants, Matthews observed over 70 percent of the participants who employed accountability either completely accomplished their goals or were over halfway there, compared to 35 percent of those whose goals existed solely in their minds (without communicating or writing them down).

Because of my commitment to this calling and vision, I knew I needed to be held accountable, so I told the world about it. In March 2017, I hopped on Facebook Live to boldly share my vision and create some accountability.

As much as I would love to say it was executed seamlessly and grandly in absolute perfection, the reality is: I was a hot mess. I rambled on about this vision I had, what I wanted to create, and why. I held up a check for $1,000,000 I had written to myself dated on my thirty-fifth birthday.

It was a mess. I was disorganized. I ugly cried. I wrapped the video, shut down all my social media, turned off my phone, and left the house. What had I just done? I had no idea if I got my message across. I had no idea how people would react.

Luckily none of it mattered. The point of doing it was to put it out in the world. It wasn't about anyone else. It was about taking a stand for my commitment and getting into alignment. It was about making myself accountable because now there were other people enrolled in my vision. On the days I had the slightest urge to turn back, I knew I would have to explain it to my friends and community.

I encourage you to find a way to move your vision from inside you to outside you. It doesn't have to be massive and grand; the most important part is that it's done. Confide in a colleague, a trusted friend, a coach, or a mentor. Find a safe community with whom to share it (if I may, the Permission to Leap community on Facebook is a great option!).

Your brain will think you're dying. You'll see saber-toothed tigers everywhere. You could get perfection paralysis. You will want to procrastinate. As my friend Amy Birks says, "You are going to want to vomit."

Don't allow your fear of a less-than-perfect delivery hinder you. And more than anything don't let the anticipated judgments from others prevent you from doing it. This shit isn't supposed to be easy, but it is supposed to create for us a life we are proud to live.

Remember why you got off the fence in the first place. Allow that to be your guiding force. Instead of assuming it's going to go horribly, why not assume it will go perfectly?

Here's the deal: as much as we'd all love to do big things in the world without fear, it's never going to happen. I hear so many reflections from women that they need to "conquer" their fears before they take action. If that's what you're waiting for, you will be waiting a long fucking time.

Leaps involve fear. Period.

In fact, as my good friend Ashley Cooper recently said to me, "When you're about to do something great, fear will never be more present."

It's not about the absence of fear, it's about finding the strength within to remember your fears are not real; they are simply markers that you're on the right path. And it's about embracing the confidence to choose your vision despite the fear.

How will you choose to take a stand for your vision?

ARE YOU CRAZY?

Pause. There is a very important part of your declaration I have only briefly touched upon, a part you may have overlooked if you weren't paying full attention: find a safe community with whom to share it.

There are going to be people in your sphere who do not support your leap. There will be people who think you're crazy, people who want to talk you out of your desires, and people who flat-out attack you.

They will reflect back to you all your fears about the leap and point out all the reasons you should stay where you are. A lot of the people you talk to will want to know how this is going to happen or what your plan is. They may poke holes in your vision. Before writing this book, I even had someone laugh and say, "I'll believe it when I see it."

Being seen and taking a stand for your vision opens you up to persecution.

And now, not only are you dealing with your own inner doubts, fears, and hesitations, you have to deal with other people's issues as well.

Here's the good news: most of their reactions have nothing to do with you. Again, the correct perspective is not that you've made the wrong decision; it's simply that your decision makes them uncomfortable or they don't currently exist in the vibration of your vision.

Their reaction does not mean you've made the wrong decision. In fact, 99.9 percent of the time, their reaction has nothing to do with you. Their reaction has everything to do with them. Your willingness to birth your vision can trigger jealousy, fears, and feelings of unworthiness and inadequacy in others. It may reveal to them their inability to say "yes" to getting off the fence. It may show them the fears keeping their life in a holding pattern.

And, if you're not careful and you do allow their perspectives, opinions, and fears to permeate you,it will only compound and trigger your own fears more and more. Let the people around you take responsibility and ownership for their own feelings and reactions. It's not your burden to bear.

> "People will love you. People will
> hate you. And none of it will have
> anything to do with you."
> Abraham Hicks

My public declaration of my vision on Facebook triggered several people in my life. I received a few incredulous messages and phone calls along the lines of: Who was I to think I could say such a thing? Why did I think I was so special to earn that kind of result? How could I be so narcissistic to make a video declaring my desire to own a million-dollar company?

For the most part, I lovingly and patiently allowed each person to have their own experience with my vision. I won't lie—I nearly took responsibility for a few. There were some that cut to the bone and really hurt. But one of the messages I received reminded me of the truth:

"When I was watching your video, I could definitely feel your vulnerability and that triggered within me the things I have been ignoring to be vulnerable with myself. I cried inconsolably while watching your video and after, for part of the morning and afternoon. It felt good to cry. It felt good to realize that I can change it, but only if I face it, change my beliefs around those situations and take actions to make things better. Your video pushed me. It gave me that huge nudge that I've needed these past couple of weeks. It was fucking uncomfortable, but I didn't ignore it and I am glad I didn't. I just let myself feel everything. That pain that was brought to the surface the day when you went live helped me open up to things that I had been ignoring. I needed that kick in the butt with being triggered to focus on how I want to make an impact again through my gifts and talents."

There will be people who disagree with your vision, who attack you for your vision, and who stop talking to you because of your vision. I wish I could tell you it's all sunshine, puppies, and rainbows. This is a hard reality that comes along with both personal growth work and fulfilling your commitment to your leap.

So how do you move past other people's judgment? How do you protect yourself from the projections others will try to place upon you?

It's easy to say, "Oh, just ignore them." But what happens when they're your family or best friends?

Remember, their judgment and projections are only your problem if you allow them to be your problem. Instead of allowing their words to hold weight or truth in your life, why not use their words to teach yourself deeper self-acceptance? Why not allow their words to guide you to areas to strengthen your inner resolve?

You must find a way to navigate their issues while keeping your light protected. Use your daily practice to strengthen your foundation. Instead of looking to their perceptions, judgments, and criticisms, look to your truth. Stand on the foundation you have built. And more than anything, lean on why you said "yes" to your leap in the first place. Allow it to be your North Star.

And send them compassion. So much compassion.

Last year I spoke with a colleague about the shift in relationships that happens when one decides to leap into life changes. He explained to me how he sees the changes we experience in our relationships as a result of a commitment to growth:

"Bri, it's like you're on an elevator. When you were younger, it was filled with all the friends from your elementary and high school days. When your elevator ascends to college, some of the people on your elevator get off. You continue going up little by little, and at every floor you stop on, some people get off and some new people get on. When you are experiencing rapid growth, like you are, there will be a mass exodus of people off your elevator. For a period of time, it might just be you and one or two other people. It's not because they don't love you. It's because they can't handle the energy and vibrations of moving farther and farther up."

People are going to get off your elevator. They will self-select out of your life because it's no longer aligned for them to continue forward on your journey with you. Heck, you may even need to kick people off your elevator. That's not to say these people need to be eradicated from your life, maybe just that your relationship needs to evolve.

The good news about all this is while there will be people who are no longer vibrationally aligned with you, there will also be new people who enter your elevator who are aligned and want to support you in your growth.

Gary Temple Bodley writes in *A Radical Change in Your Approach to Life*, "You will be aligned [to friendships] with those to which you are vibrationally compatible. As you raise your vibration by living consciously, you will meet many new people who also vibrate at this level. There is never anything to be worried about. If you were not a vibrational match you would not meet. ... You are moving up and they are there to greet you."

Your realignment will come in many forms following your commitment. Your job is to be in flow with what comes up, release what's no longer serving you, and trust the Spiritual World is rearranging things in divine perfection to support your vision coming to life.

And, of course, don't forget to grab yourself a copy of my "Future-Self Meditation" to meet, connect with, and learn about your future self at http://permissiontoleap.today.

7. Envision Your Successful Leap

Completing the "Future-Self Meditation" is just the tip of the iceberg. Once you have gained the new perspective of your future, it's important to continue accessing this feeling and this energy on a regular basis. Doing it once and then returning to your current perspective is not enough to create the necessary alignment shift.

Persistent application of your future frequency and perspective is necessary to eliminate the perceived separation of the present and the future. It increases your clarity and enables you to see everything through the eyes of your future, causing the Spiritual World to have no option but to start putting the pieces of the puzzle together. Little by little, bits and pieces of the next steps will be revealed.

In the last chapter, we talked about releasing things that are out of alignment, but now it's time to welcome what is in alignment and allow that to carry you forward to each next step.

Visualization is an incredibly powerful tool to support you in this.

WHAT IS VISUALIZATION?

Visualization is a process of creating a situation, action, or experience in your mind without actually performing it physically. It's using imagery in your mind to simulate what you want to experience in your life.

HOW DOES IT WORK?

When you imagine something, your brain processes it in the same manner as it would if you were performing the activity. For example, if you envision yourself driving a car, it stimulates the same area of the brain stimulated when actually driving a car. Envisioning an action or situation activates your brain in the same manner as performing the action or experiencing the situation.

A study performed in 2004 analyzed the brain patterns in weight lifters (Ranganathan, et al. 2004). It found that the brain patterns activated when they lifted weights were also activated when the weight lifters simply imagined the activity. Our application of mental imagery impacts the cognitive processes in our brain such as motor controls, attention, perception, planning, and memory.

The thalamus, a processor in our brain, is what receives input from our senses and motor signals. It not only receives the information, but it also processes and relays 98 percent of what we experience in the rest of the brain. The thalamus does not differentiate between our Physical World and what we imagine, so the information it processes and relays to the brain is categorized as if you were physically performing the action.

WHAT HAPPENS AFTER CONTINUOUS AND SUSTAINED VISUALIZATION?

Our brain is like a superhighway. We have 100 billion neurons within our brain transmitting information to our nerves, muscles, and glands. Through trillions of pathways in our brain, these neurons communicate and deliver their messages. After years and years and years of transmitting the same signals, the pathways connecting your regular, daily thoughts and actions are well-worn.

In the beginning, visualization may require a large amount of effort because you are introducing new thoughts and beliefs into your superhighway, and your brain wants to stick to the pathways it knows. It is possible to create new pathways for your brain to communicate, but it does not happen overnight.

Right now, the pathway to your vision does not exist in your head. It's up to you to create it.

When you visualize your desired result over and over again, it becomes reality for your brain. Consistent visualization of the imagery you desire strengthens your pathways and enables you to perceive your result as "normal." Each time you envision your desired result, you reinforce the path to the result, which only increases your motivation to execute this vision but also heightens your potential for success in achieving your vision.

In 2008, sixty-four medical students, all in their second year of medical school, were put to the test (Sanders, et al. 2008). Each student was randomly assigned to one of two treatment groups. The first undertook mental imagery, and the second were given textbooks. Both groups received the same course, including lectures, demonstrations, and physical practice, but the groups were divided with the additional training between textbook study and visualization.

Over the period of the study, the students' progress was measured on three different occasions. The analysis of the results revealed a significant difference in abilities between the two groups. The group assigned to visualization consistently performed better in actual surgeries than the textbook group.

You can use visualization from the smallest things, like a phone call you're dreading or waking up refreshed, to the biggest things like landing on the other side of your leap!

Visualization transfers to the real world. Guang Yue, a psychologist from the Cleveland Clinic Foundation in Ohio, compared "people who went to the gym with people who carried out virtual workouts in their heads" (Ranganathan, et al. 2004). His study found that people who went to the gym and performed physical activity increased their muscle mass by 30 percent, and the group who never went to the gym, and instead simply visualized, increased their muscle mass by 13.5 percent.

If you can get results by visualization alone, and you can get results from physical application alone, imagine what could happen if you were to combine the two.

That's exactly what Olympian Michael Phelps has done. In addition to spending hours and hours in the pool each day, when he was twelve years old, he began to visualize the perfect swim.

It was the last thing he did each night before falling asleep, and it was the first thing he did each morning when he woke up. Phelps would envision himself on the starting block, jumping off, swimming perfect laps, and finishing the race.

He particularly noted the sensations and muscle strain of each stroke and each turn. He touched the walls of the pool with his mind. He perceived the water rushing and dripping off his face as he crested the water to rip off his goggles and look at the clock as he finished.

Phelps lay in bed, night after night and morning after morning, playing this mental picture until he knew every second of it by heart. By the time he touched the Olympic pool, he'd already experienced the race thousands of times.

When Phelps qualified for the Olympic team in 2000, he was the youngest male to make the team in sixty-eight years. In 2004, he walked away from the Olympic Games with six gold and two bronze medals, but it wasn't until 2008 that his visualization skills were really put to the test.

Phelps prepared for the 200-meter butterfly race in the same way he prepared for all races. The start of the race was business as usual. He stood behind the starting block, bounced on his toes, got onto the block, swung his arms, assumed the stance, and leapt into the water when the gun sounded. But the second his face hit the water, he knew this would not be a normal race.

His goggles did not fully seal to his face, and little by little, water leaked in, impairing his vision. By the third turn, Phelps was swimming completely blind. His goggles were full of water.

Phelps relied on his tens of thousands of visual practices to get him through to the end. He had performed this swim so many times already he didn't need to rely on his sense of sight. Instead of backing off and conceding defeat, Phelps increased his force midway through the final lap and began counting his strokes.

Eighteen.

Nineteen.

Twenty.

Just one more.

On his twenty-first stroke, he touched the wall. Not only had Phelps won another gold medal, when he ripped off his goggles and set his eyes on the scoreboard, he learned he had also set a world record. When Phelps was later asked how it felt to swim blind, he responded, "Just like I imagined it would. If I didn't prepare for everything that happens, when my goggles started filling up, I'd have probably flipped out. That's why I swim in the dark."

Phelps' coach, Bob Bowman, published his book *The Golden Rules* in 2016. It shares ten steps for excellence in all walks of life, including his encouragement of visualization techniques. "The most strongly held mental picture is where you'll be … so get really good at mental rehearsal," Bowman instructs. "If you can form a strong mental picture and visualize yourself doing it, your brain will immediately find ways to get you there."

It was under Bowman's guidance that Phelps began his twice-daily visualization practices. In preparation for races, Bowman encourages him to increase his practice—not just in, but also out of the pool. "For months before a race Michael gets into a relaxed state. He mentally rehearses for two hours a day. He sees himself winning. He smells the air, tastes the water, hears the sounds, and sees the clock."

Bowman knows this mental rehearsal is just as important as the physical practice. "The brain cannot distinguish between something that's vividly imagined and something that's real."

While this practice is common in athletes and high-performance people, it's one you can incorporate into your daily life to support you in creating what it is you desire as well.

VISUALIZATION LEADS TO CLARITY

The more you can use visualization to connect and align with your goal, the more the next steps on your journey will be revealed. Clarity is a natural by-product of visualization.

Let me share a few small tricks to achieving it.

Our ego loves to get involved with the visualization process. It begins to "should" all over our desires and/or compares what we want with those around us, and before we know it, our vision has taken on a life of its own almost unrecognizable from what we actually desire.

A great way to keep this from happening is to continually ask yourself "why." Why do I want this? Why is this aspect of my vision important to me? If your desires are rooted in what other people have, the lives they are living, what people desire for your life, the expectations of society, or any other sort of comparison, it's not your vision because those things stem from the Physical World.

In order to visualize, one must step into the Spiritual World, which means relinquishing the need to control, push, force, or manipulate and instead, surrender and allow. The most powerful, aligned vision will be guided from your heart, in consideration of your values, and filled with things that bring you the utmost visceral joy. This is an opportunity to get to know yourself on an even deeper level.

Do you know your top five values that drive you in life? If not, now is a great time to understand what they are because they can help you see the underlying motivation for bringing your vision to life.

Begin by writing down your ten most important values. These may include love, integrity, freedom, passion, contribution, health, impact, etc.

Now, look at the list and cross off about three you could live without. These are values that may be important but aren't critical.

Then do that again. Look at the remaining seven values and remove three more. Again, these are values that may be influential to who you are, but they're values that may be more fluid.

The remaining four values are your core values, the cornerstones of what makes you the unique person you are in the world. Begin to look at your vision through the lens of each value and ensure they are aligned.

TAKE VISUALIZATION A STEP FURTHER

Just as your vibration can repel what isn't aligned for you, your new vibration will begin to attract what is aligned for you. Visualization not only aligns you with the Spiritual World, but also with the vibration of your dream. The law of attraction is an energetic alignment technique relying heavily on visualization. It states that your inner focus and vibration will create the corresponding external results in alignment with your vision.

Most teachings around the law of attraction will tell you to focus on what you want, which, yes, can be important. However, if you truly want to become a master at this, it goes far beyond "what" you desire and taps into the deeper reasons behind it. If you focus on the feelings your vision elicits, it will be exponentially more powerful.

It's not just about envisioning your dreams; it's about allowing yourself to step into the feelings and experience them in real time as you connect with your vision. If you can experience both the mental picture and the feelings to bridge your mind, heart, and body on a consistent basis, clarity will flow.

As I was completing this book, I was teaching visualization in my *Permission to Leap* training course. I was going on about the importance of feeling your visualization, explaining it's not something that happens in your mind; visualization happens in your heart.

One of the attendees chimed in, "It sounds like it's less visual-ization and more feel-ization."

She was spot-on.

Seeing your vision as if you were watching a movie is incredibly helpful, but feeling your vision as if you were experiencing it in real time takes it to a greater level. Feeling your vision will produce the corresponding vibrations and put you directly in the frequency of what you desire.

LET GO OF YOUR NEED TO CONTROL

One crucial aspect of this is to release how your vision shows up in the Physical World. Our human mind wants to immediately start formulating plans and manipulating exactly how our vision is going to come into reality. You get a slight glimpse of what's to come, and your brain defaults to "figure it out" mode. But there is one very important thing to remember: it is your job to know what you want and why you want it, and it is the Spiritual World's job to take care of the rest.

Your leap will not happen by going into the Physical World and doing, doing, doing. As you've learned, leaps are created from the inside out. By attaching to one specific way your vision must exist in your life, you will prevent other outcomes from existing.

There is a scene in *The Matrix* when Neo is taken to the prophet to learn if he is The One. As he's in the living room waiting to be seen, he has an experience with a child sitting on the floor. This child has a spoon levitating in front of him that is in the process of bending in half. When Neo is caught observing him, the child explains the secret. "Do not try and bend the spoon. That's impossible. Instead, only try to realize the truth. … There is no spoon. Then you'll see that it is not the spoon that bends; it is only yourself."

Going straight into the physical world to get shit done is like trying to bend the spoon. Leaps and manifestation are about bending ourselves. The action and the path will come. It's up to you to trust and allow it to be revealed to you, not to force your world into submission.

At this stage, feeling into the energy of this vision will create more powerful results than sitting down to plan out your path. Logic-ing yourself into your leap does not work, and the more you dwell in this energy of logic and figuring it out, the more that clarity will elude you.

Here's a fun exercise to perform in the moments when you feel yourself trying to bend the spoon. Sit down and write out fifty different ways your dream could come to you—yes, I said fifty! Make your list, and then, the trick is to unattached yourself to the fifty ways. In fact, usually when I do this, my fiftieth item is "these or something better still."

Be creative with this. The idea behind it is to open your mind to the possibilities. It can be a mix of things that are "realistic" and things that may never happen. It doesn't matter how your vision materializes. What matters is staying open and feeling into why you want your vision to be your reality.

Here are some examples from the "Fifty Things Exercise" in the *Permission to Leap* community:

Financial Freedom/Abundance

Finding money on the street, receiving an inheritance, a surprise call from a new client, getting a raise, discovering an offshore bank account with your name on it, it's delivered by owl, get contacted by a film crew who wants to pay you to rent your home for a week, get paid to drive a friend to the airport, be asked to participate in a paid research study, take on a part-time side job, have a garage sale, etc.

Significant Other

Sit next to each other on a flight, bump into them while exiting an elevator, get introduced by a friend, stand in the morning coffee line behind them, reach for the same apple at the grocery store at the same time, meet online, get set up by a matchmaker, you end up talking at a party and they ask you out, etc.

New Job

A recruiter contacts you, a friend recommends you for a position, you overhear the person next to you at the coffee shop talking about hiring for the position you would be perfect for and strike up a conversation, you apply in all the usual routes, your current company promotes you, an old boss calls you and asks you to move to a new company with them, you see a "Help Wanted" sign and walk in, you join a community on Facebook and someone posts a job listing, etc.

Surrender into not knowing how your leap is going to reveal itself. Let go of your attachment to the tangible, sensible actions and plans. Release the need for it to come via any of the things on your list, and allow the Spiritual World to step in and turn your dreams into reality. If you get too hung up on how your vision will be created in the world, you will end up missing or overlooking it when it does show up because it will almost always arrive differently than you anticipated.

CREATE YOUR FEEL-IZATION

A few years ago, I was visiting Las Vegas with my family. On our final day in Sin City, we rented a car to visit Hoover Dam. At the time, a new bridge was being constructed over the canyon, and it was one of the coolest things I had ever seen.

At 880 feet in the air, this gigantic 1,905-foot-long bridge would eventually serve as a bypass from the outdated two-lane road. I had never seen a bridge this large under construction.

In 2009, when we were there, they were roughly halfway done constructing the arch. The thing that absolutely blew my mind was that this bridge was not being constructed from one side to the other. There were crews on each side of the canyon diligently building toward the center, which means on the left side was 25 percent of the constructed bridge, and on the right side was 25 percent of the constructed bridge.

When you're creating your leap, it's common to envision a path moving from where you are right now to where you're going at the end of your leap. But what if you could be concurrently building from both sides to meet in the middle?

I like to use visualization as if I'm building from the future and the present concurrently, as if I'm building a bridge spanning a huge chasm that meets in the middle. I see myself as the arc being constructed from one side of the canyon and my visualization stretching toward the center of the canyon from the other side. If you build from both sides, you'll meet in the middle more quickly and be able to walk the rest of the way across the chasm.

It was December 25, 2015, and I had broken up with a boyfriend who I learned was cheating on me. I was feeling very sorry for myself. In full victim mode, I left the house on Christmas morning to take advantage of the best hiking day of the year in Los Angeles. Sitting in Dante's View on Mt. Hollywood, I pulled out my journal.

My initial musings that day were colored with a "how did I get here, woe is me" energy. But then something shifted, and I began to ask myself what was important to me, what I wanted to create, and how it felt to be living that life (rather than the one I currently faced). I began to see what my life could be like post-breakup victimhood.

This is what I wrote that morning:

I wake up in my condo in Downtown Los Angeles every morning next to my love. We express our gratitude for one another then spend time creating and visioning our lives together. I use my morning routine to center and ground myself as I step into my power. Doing this helps me remember who I am in the world in order to attract and manifest my desires with ease and receive clarity from source. My workday is varied but always flows with inspired action to create aligned results and generate my financial goals every month. I love working from my dream office as it fuels my passion and creativity. My practice is full, with clients who are creating epic results and easily increasing their success in the world. I have a book agent who is helping me finish Volume 2 of the Inspirational Woman Project. The relationships in my business and personal lives continually fill me up. I am surrounded by powerful, inspired beings who are completely badass and wonderfully supportive. These relationships are filled with integrity, love and laughter. Evenings are a blend between intimate and quiet connection time, adventures with loved ones and community expansion. I am completely fulfilled. My heart is so happy. My soul is on purpose. I am so supported.

After writing it down, I broke out my cell phone and opened the voice recorder app to dictate the entire vision.

The next morning, I woke up to my alarm, rolled over, and hit play to hear my voice tell me about all the amazingness of my life. Day after day, for months on end, I listened to this same recording from bed and initiated my days immersed in the energy of feeling into my vision.

At some point, I stopped listening to it. Life got in the way, my routine was thrown off, and I discarded it to the wayside.

Fast-forward to August 15, 2016. I pull out my journal while waiting for dinner at an outdoor cafe in Los Feliz. It was a rare night to be eating out, but it was necessary because my entire home was packed at the time, waiting for the movers to arrive the following day to relocate me to my dream place in Downtown Los Angeles.

I flipped the pages, looking over the last eight months of my life, when I stopped on the original vision I had written.

Holy. Shit. This was my life.

OK, well, not 100 percent. But it was mostly my life.

I was moving the following day. My business was thriving more than it ever had with a huge influx of powerful clients. The relationships in my life were phenomenal. I had my dream office and my book agent. My income had quadrupled. I had successfully shown up for my daily practice all year.

I was dying. This shit works!

I listened to the same recording for at least five months and used it to feel into the vision as if it were reality, which had literally transformed my life into what I desired. I immediately turned to the first blank page to write out another vision.

Here are some great questions to ask yourself when preparing your feel-ization:

What excites you about your vision?

> • Why does what you are doing and/or creating matter to you and others? How do you feel when you're in this state?

> • Who are the most important people in your life? Why do they matter to you? What kind of interactions do you have with them? What do you talk about? How do you feel around them?

> • What places are you experiencing every day? Why do they excite you? How do you feel in these places?

> • What's your home life like? How do you feel in your home? What's most important to you about your home?

> • How does it feel to fully express your talents in the world? Why do your talents matter to the world?

Here are a few extra tips to use when writing your vision:

> 1. Write from the present. You want to listen to, see, and experience it as if it is your reality in this moment (not in some future time).

> 2. Focus less on things and focus more on feelings. If you write the letter with so much specificity, it can actually prevent your vision from manifesting into your reality.

3. Write from a place of abundance. Avoid the phrase "at least" and add a plus sign after each number.

4. Focus on what you want to bring into your life and not on what you don't. For example, if part of your vision is to get out of debt, you actually want to focus on financial freedom because saying you want to get out of debt, your focus is on the debt—and what you focus on grows.

Need more support around writing your vision? Be sure to grab these tips and more in the worksheet online at http://permissiontoleap.today.

Now it's time for you to write your vision and use it for your feel-ization practice! Remember, the more you can connect with the feelings of it, the more powerful it will be. Don't just write your vision—make a plan to read, draw, or listen to your vision every day. Who knows … maybe someday you'll have your own version of twenty-three Olympic gold medals.

8. The Universal Double-Check

As I mentioned in Chapter 5, my life in Olympia, Washington was increasing in pain and frustration year after year. I was depressed and didn't recognize the woman I had become. Plus, Olympia was only supposed to be a temporary resting place. What had begun as a three-month commitment spawned a seven-year residency (complete with home ownership!), and it just didn't work any longer. My fashion business was expanding little by little and I hated my day job more and more. I needed out.

I was seven months deep into my leap to leave Olympia. For seven full months, I planned and schemed about my escape from the gray of the Pacific Northwest, envisioning my life and all the possibilities awaiting me in Chicago, Phoenix, New York, and Los Angeles.

In those seven months I had (unknowingly) gone through all the stages of the leap: deciding what was most important to me, jumping off the fence, talking to people about the move, and getting into alignment. I was so aligned that clarity kicked in, and I zeroed my sights on the City of Angels as my destination.

The ball was rolling. The momentum was palpable. I could taste the excitement.

To ensure I didn't back out, I continuously packed a box or two per week since the moment of my commitment. My garage was bursting with box after box of my belongings—so much so my car wouldn't fit.

I was all in, or so I thought. And with my self-imposed deadline to move looming a mere ten weeks in the future, Mama Seeley came to visit.

It was a standard mom visit—cooking nourishing food, kitty time, exploring sights and sewing—up until the last day.

"I don't think it's a good idea to move."

I could feel the instant panic set into my throat and stomach. "What?"

"I worry. Los Angeles is a big city. It's scary. What if something happens? You're my little girl. You have an amazing job and community here. Maybe you should just move to Seattle and then travel more often for your business."

Now, to be fair, she wasn't saying anything new. I was already internally experiencing all these thoughts and fears. But hearing the words spoken aloud in the Physical World was entirely new—and from my mom, no less. There was something about hearing my fears voiced by someone else, outside my own brain, which made them so much more real.

This was a woman who supported all my crazy ideas, including going to college four hours away from home a year early without having toured the school. She barely questioned me moving to Italy without knowing the language or a single soul. She was the one who pulled up the Internet and told me where Olympia was located after I accepted a job there. And while she often posed questions to help provide clarity and discernment, I couldn't recall a time where she took a hard stand in opposition to a life change I was so invested in.

I was so invested, in fact, I had stopped paying my mortgage to be eligible for a short sale; I was ready to walk away from my first home.

THIS MUST BE A SIGN!!!

The Universe must be speaking directly to me through my mom to let me know what a terrible idea this is. Yeah, that's it. It's totally a sign.

This small conversation catapulted me into a mental battle of epic proportions. The pendulum swung moment by moment between the extremes of staying in the safety of what I knew and the complete upheaval of my normal to reestablish myself in Los Angeles. I vacillated between living in discord with my soul's desire to be in a more vibrant surrounding to an intense impulse to throw what I could fit in my car, drive away, and never look back.

Day after day, this inner anguish tore me apart. Move or don't move. Stay or go. Commit or bail.

Even though I had been preparing for this for seven months and thought I was 110 percent in, the reality was I still had escape's phone number on speed dial. I could wake up tomorrow and, with a grand "just kidding," let it all disappear.

Yes, I'd have to face my disappointment and the embarrassment. Yes, I'd have to answer all the questions about why I didn't go. Yes, I'd have to heal my broken heart.

But it wouldn't be so scary. I could cozy up in my comfort zone, pull my curtains to close out the gray, curl up with the kitties on my lap, and ignore the scream for expansion raging in my head all hours of the night and day. I could be OK staying here.

After all, Olympia was my happy place for seven years. I had a community here. My public profile increased significantly, and my designs were being recognized. It would be easier to stay.

The week following Mama Seeley's visit, I boarded a flight to Los Angeles. I booked my ticket months earlier to watch my sister Makayla sing live for the very first time on her choir tour. Not to mention, it was a brilliant move on my past self's part to help me explore my soon-to-be future self's new home.

While my past self could never have anticipated the conundrum in which I found myself, this trip was exactly what I needed to get off the fence once and for all. It was a do-or-die trip. I was either going to return to Washington to finish packing and move to Los Angeles, or I was going to start looking for a new place to live in Seattle (because if I was staying in Washington, it would still mean selling my house and would definitely require moving to a larger city).

I arrived in Los Angeles to brilliant February weather (much different from the rainstorm I faced on the drive to SeaTac airport). I acquired my rental car, drove to my Airbnb, and, having arrived too early, walked to Silverlake Reservoir with yoga mat and journal in hand.

What do I want? Why was it so difficult to answer this simple question without all the pros and cons getting in the way? That day, sitting under the sun, I wanted a simple answer, yet none came. Or, at least, no answer came immediately or in the way I was expecting.

My days on that trip were filled with sunshine, new and old friends, grilled cheese, explorations, sightseeing, and more. It was on this trip that I confirmed my roommate and found two women to share my office. This exploration led me to discover which neighborhood was right for me to live in. And it was with my toes in the sand, watching the sunset over the Pacific Ocean, I recommitted to my vision.

The answer to "What do I want?" had not presented itself in an immediate, declarative way because the entire trip was my answer: the rays of sun on my skin, the laughter shared with friends, the opportunities lining up seamlessly, and the grilled cheese.

I returned to Washington with the escape hatch closed once and for all. I was ready to burn the bridge leading back to my old life with only one option ahead—moving to Los Angeles. My Universal double-check moment enabled me to remember why I committed to my leap in the first place and why, no matter how many fears I possessed, it was still my top priority.

Once I did this, everything fell into place quicker than I thought possible. Two short days after leaving LA, I got a call from my new roommate, Lamar. "I found our new home. It's everything."

"Wait—I thought you said you weren't impulsive about this stuff."

"I'm not. But there I was, on our amazing new rooftop with a 360° unobstructed view of the city, looking around and taking in the sights, when the heavens opened up. As I looked to my right, the clouds parted in perfect timing to allow a beam of light through, and it was that light that perfectly illuminated the Hollywood sign as my gaze landed on it. I told the manager we'd take it."

Less than three weeks later, I was pulling into town with a full car and two terrified kitties ... ready to make Los Angeles my home.

ARE YOU REALLY SURE?

This is the stage of the leap where things get real. You've been thinking and talking about your leap, but at this point it's still just an idea. And the possibility of getting out still exists.

This is the moment the Universe gives you one last opportunity to decide if this change is really what you want. It's a time when your feet get put to the flames and you answer once and for all—do you really want this?

I first learned about this concept in 2015 as the "Universal Double-Check."

What is the "Universal Double-Check?" It's the last assurance you're committed. It's the final fork in the road to ensure the changes coming your way are what you choose. It is the final deciding point just before the energy existing in the Spiritual World reveals itself in the Physical World.

Before things begin to materialize in the Physical World, it's important to have this final decisive moment. Once your outer world begins shifting, it's harder for things to reverse themselves when they have taken on a physical form versus when it's just energy and ideas.

The Universal Double-Check happens to everyone, in every leap, all the time.

• A friend decides to move out of LA. All of the sudden everything begins to pick up for her—her business is thriving, she's meeting amazing people, and life is ideal.

• We make the decision to close our podcast, and we not only experience our biggest month (150 percent growth), but it's also our largest day of downloads to date (nearly double our previous record).

• You decide to leave your significant other and suddenly your relationship is on point—there are easy conversations, supportive vibes, and you start remembering all the good times.

I see the Universal Double-Check like renewing vows.

The initial commitment is a bit easier: you haven't gotten into the process and may not even know what you're getting into. But now you've experienced more. Your vision may have been tested, or you faced challenges to cause you to question it. The road may have been a bit rocky up until this point. Now you get to decide if you have the faith to continue and trust in what's to come.

The conversation between Mama Seeley and I that I convinced myself was a "sign," was nothing more than the Universe showing me I still had a choice. I could choose safety and comfort. I could choose to let my fears dictate my outcome. It wasn't an indication or warning I shouldn't do it; it was simply a question of "are you sure?" just before everything began to click into place.

Oftentimes we mistake the Universal Double-Check as a why we should not leap. We take it as a sign we're on the wrong path when, in fact, it's simply an opportunity to strengthen our commitment to our vision. Remember: this is just an outer reflection of the fears, doubts, and hesitation already in existence within you. It's the Physical World reflecting what exists under the surface of the Spiritual World.

The Universal Double-Check commonly reveals itself in a few different ways. The first is through friends and family, the people closest to us, the ones we are more likely to listen to what they have to say. They're also the most likely to trigger our fears and doubts. We can brush off the opinions of strangers, but we listen when the message is coming from a trusted source. It may be presented in the form of concern for you taking this step, or it could come up as anger or resentment.

When I received the messages after making my million-dollar-business declaration, there were some very real moments when I questioned whether they were right. Who did I think I was to want this? How dare I make such a bold statement of my desires? My ego was clearly running the show. I needed to take down my video and just pretend it didn't happen.

Except then I got quiet. I went into my bedroom and settled into my meditation chair with my fur baby Peechez on my lap. In that silence and space, I was able to reconnect with my heart and myself. What was my truth? Did I make this declaration to harm other people? Was I following this vision from a place of ego?

While resting my mind, I received a very clear visual of ripples moving out from my body. I looked down in my meditation to see myself standing in a shallow pool of water. As each ripple moved out from my body, another woman would appear in the water with me. And another. And another. I was entirely surrounded by women. We were standing elbow-to-elbow for miles. I saw nothing but women, and in my heart I felt the expansion as the ripples continued to touch one woman, and then the next and the next and the next for as far as the eye could see.

The Universe was providing me the opportunity to look at whether or not I was truly committed to my leap. I was presented with the vision of what was possible—reaching and impacting woman after woman and creating this ripple effect in the world. This meditation revealed that while this was my leap, this leap wasn't about me. And if I decided to let this Universal Double-Check get the best of me, these women would be deprived of the expansion I was on the planet to share with them.

I left my meditative state and reentered the Physical World with complete peace. This was the right leap for me to take in this moment.

Jessica Tang explained her Universal Double-Check on the Permission to Leap Podcast:

"After deciding to invest in coaching with Bri for six months, I spoke with one of my girlfriends about it. She's definitely not an entrepreneur, having taken a very traditional route in life.

"I told her about the investment I had chosen to make, which was met with her worry and concern. I told her, 'I appreciate your concern but I feel like this is right.' Her boyfriend, who I'm also really close to, ended up calling me personally to say, 'Hey Jess, I don't think this is a good idea.'

"I was really taken aback by that. I found myself getting really defensive during that phone call, so much so that I actually had to say, 'Hey, I love you, and I really appreciate you showing your love to me this way but I'm feeling like I can't really continue this conversation until after I've calmed down a little bit. I want you to trust me. I know you love me, but I need you to trust me. I know what I'm doing.'

"I knew that he was coming from a place of love, although it was also a place of fear. He was scared that I was going to get into this huge level of debt that I couldn't dig myself out of.

"That was a really tough conversation. We had another conversation at a later date. He called me and said, 'I'm sorry. I didn't really mean to come across as judgmental. I love you. I'm just scared for you.' I responded, 'I'm scared too.'

"But despite being scared, I knew it was right. I knew there was a lot of healing I had to face within myself in order to be a better and more successful entrepreneur. It's really interesting because one of the biggest issues that was stopping me from being as successful as I wanted to be was my actual fear of money, fear of talking about money. The experience of answering questions from my friends and facing their fears actually helped me heal my fear of money, or of asking people for money in exchange for my services."

Jessica's experience with her Universal Double-Check not only enabled her to recommit to her vision on a deeper level, but it allowed her to go toe-to-toe with her fears around money to begin healing them.

Another way the Universal Double-Check may show up in your life is an out-of-the-blue opportunity in complete alignment with your current life, but drastically out of alignment with your vision. This could be anything from a job offer or promotion, to a home refinance, to an investor, to a high-paying client or a spike in numbers, etc.

Every time I was fed up with my day job and considered quitting, I'd get notice I was receiving a raise or that they would work with me in adjusting my schedule to work fewer hours. It never failed. So I continued to say "yes" to staying at my day job despite the pain I was experiencing inside each day. After all, a raise or schedule negotiation had to be a sign I should stay, right?

One of my colleagues was in the midst of building her dream. She was moving through the alignment area, getting clarity, and taking action. I could see the shifts in her week by week, even though she was having a hard time seeing them for herself. She was frustrated and impatient. Her results weren't coming fast enough in the Physical World, and she wasn't spending any time connecting with the Spiritual World. One day over coffee she shared with me that she was giving up her dream. A job recruiter from her old occupation reached out with the perfect job. She'd had through several interviews and accepted the position, and a few weeks later, her business was no longer.

This story always reminds me of the meme of a miner digging a tunnel. What he doesn't know is he is just one more swing away from hitting gold, but because he's been working for so long without reward, he gives up. Had he just stuck with it for one more swing of the axe, all of his work would have paid off.

A third way the Universal Double-Check could pop up in your life is through a life-altering event or experience. My car accident was absolutely a Universal Double-Check. I spent months moaning about my life, feeling exhausted, and being unclear of what to do about it. Then over a course of a few days, I attended a workshop, felt an energetic breath of fresh air, and committed to working with a coach. My life did a complete 180-degree turn from seeing a brick wall in the form of my fashion brand ahead of me to the possibility surrounding me. In that moment, I was presented with a question, "Are you sure you want to move forward with this new vision?"

As you know, I made a great amount of space that day to be sure I was asking for. On my yoga mat, I turned immediately to the Spiritual World to face my fears and decide once and for all what was going to shape my future.

BUT, HOW DO YOU KNOW?

The only way to move forward from here is to get brutally honest with yourself.

Your brain is going to want to default back to logic. What makes sense? What are the pros and the cons? What are all the risks? You are welcome to revisit all of these things by reevaluating the risk again and again and again.

But instead, I recommend setting aside your list of pros and cons and placing the majority of your focus on the important questions, such as: What do I really want? What are my values? How do I want to feel?

Why? Because your answer isn't on a logical list. It's more likely your leap doesn't make sense. Leaps rarely make sense to our rational brain in the Physical World. There is never a good time. Are you willing to trust that your desire to leap in the world means now is exactly the right time?

Sarah Biggers, founder of the beauty brand Clove + Hallow, shared with me the catalyst that pushed her past her tipping point. "I sat on the idea for a while, stuck in a position of focusing on all the obstacles to launching this business. There's never a perfect time. Yes, there are certainly better times than others, but there will always [be] some reason to cling to that keeps you from committing. You have to be honest about why you're not doing it. My personal experience was to look at and think about life in that moment and realize that as I get older, life gets more complicated. In that moment, I was the youngest, most carefree, and irresponsible that I could be. In that moment my risk tolerance was the highest that it could ever be, and I realized it was the time I should commit to that risk and go for it." This decision to embrace her vision and move forward without fully knowing the path is what has enabled her to successfully birth Clove + Hallow, and it is the same thing supporting her in reaching her long-term vision of making safe, cruelty-free, vegan beauty products mainstream.

Get out of your head and into your heart. Your brain will always come up with a million reasons why you should back out, but your head only ever speaks to you from your current reality. Your heart will always tell you the truth, and it speaks to you from a place of possibility.

A true Universal Double-Check is not a sign directing you toward the escape hatch. It's not telling you you're on the wrong path. It's simply an opportunity to reignite and recommit to your vision. It is your final chance to say "I'm in" to lock your heart to move in the direction of your dreams.

The more you are drawn and guided by something bigger than you during your leap, the better. Let your vision be a beacon of light, and use it to remind you every day why you've chosen it. Approaching your leap from a logical place will keep your perspective narrow, and it will continuously cycle you into the limited thinking of, "But I don't know how it's going to happen."

Your vision is never actually about the thing you desire. It's always about something much, much deeper. Revisit your feel-ization to connect with your values, feelings, and motivation behind your leap. Allow it to guide you as you navigate your Universal Double-Check moment.

Are you truly committed to releasing what you've known in order to create what you desire?

PLAYING ADULT DRESS UP

Just like my story about relocating to Los Angeles, when I'm facing a Universal Double-Check moment, I use it as an opportunity to dive deeper into my commitment. My favorite way to do this is to play adult dress up, which is essentially taking your feel-ization practice and acting it out in the Physical World.

Experiencing your vision will help you definitively know what is true for you and what is your (or other people's) fear. It will help you get out of your head and begin to viscerally feel the reality of your vision in your body.

Let's jump back quickly to my car accident. Remember how my car crumpled before my very eyes? Well, what I didn't tell you is I was playing adult dress up and shopping for cars for months prior to the accident.

It was January 2015, and I was driving my little Pontiac Vibe for eight years. This car took me everywhere—from Washington to South Dakota, down to California several times, and all over Los Angeles for two years. It was a great car, and I had so much love for it.

And yet, as I drove up to the Andaz Hotel to valet my car that morning, I couldn't help but feel I was outgrowing it, but I wasn't in a financial place to commit to a car payment. So I buried the thought and proceeded on with my day—except it just kept returning to my consciousness.

So when a guy I was dating casually mentioned he was going car shopping the following weekend, I invited myself along to play adult dress up.

I rode shotgun as he test-drove the Audi R8 convertible, allowing the joy to wash over me, similarly to how the wind was racing over my skin. I soaked in the sunshine as I sunk into the buttery leather seats. My smile grew with each gear change.

And when we arrived at the Aston Martin dealership, I relished the experience of two men whisking the doors open while a third waited inside with my favorite Starbucks drink in hand. I allowed myself to receive the hospitality as I was led into the James Bond–themed backroom. I listened intently as our guide described the hand-stitched leather interior and honored the 300 hours of craftsmanship that go into building each car.

Cars were never my thing. What I drove or didn't drive was of no importance to me—until I began to realize I felt like an entirely different woman when I experienced life with such joy and playful receptivity. It's not the cars that mattered. What was important was the woman I got to be in the experience. Simply being her, I shifted my frequency so much that the Physical World had no choice but to come into alignment with what I had created in the Spiritual World.

Playing adult dress up is allowing yourself to experience the thoughts and feelings of your future self while viscerally touching the life you want to be living. Here are some examples of ways you can play adult dress up:

- Want to travel often? Have coffee or sit by the pool of a local hotel while being the kind of person who travels frequently.

- Want to be in a relationship? Take yourself out for dinner while acting, feeling, and experiencing it as if you were with your future partner.

- Want to have a private driver? Grab a Lyft and feel what it is like to have someone drive you around.

- Want to be your own boss? See if there were a way your current job would allow you to work remotely one day a week.

- Want to have a child? Offer to babysit for a friend, or go to the store and window shop as if you were preparing for your child to arrive.

- Want a new car? Test-drive your dream cars and speak with an agent.

• Want to start a charity to serve the underprivileged in a foreign country? Volunteer at your local shelter.

One of the most common issues I hear about this is, "I can't afford to live as if. My future self has money and I don't have any money, so how can I go experience the life I want to have?" This experience does not require you to spend any money whatsoever. The importance of living as if is to feel the feelings and experience as if it were your reality.

If your future self gets regular manicures and you can't currently afford to purchase that experience, create it for yourself at home and feel the way you would as if you were in the salon. If you want to meet a partner who takes you out for dinner yet you can't afford to take yourself out for dinner, then make yourself an amazing meal, put a second place setting on the table so while you eat, you experience it as if you were eating out across from your love. There is always a way to live as if regardless of how close it is to your vision.

The truth is, in that moment your "live as if" becomes your reality. The only thing separating your "live as if" from your vision is your perception of it. Instead of telling yourself, "This is just a test, not my real life," what if you were to allow yourself to be fully immersed in it? Once you are steeped in the energy of your vision, your answer to the Universal Double-Check will reveal itself, just like it did for me when I visited Los Angeles on that final occasion before moving.

9. Take the Leap

The stage has been set. Your inner work to strengthen your commitment, increase your confidence, and receive clarity has all been leading up to this moment. It's time to leap.

Except it seems as if nothing is happening. In fact, it's as if less is happening now than through the entire leap process. Isn't this supposed to be the moment when the upswing happens and everything takes off?

Yes and no. There is always a momentary pause just before this happens.

It's the moment skydiving when you get to the edge of the plane and sit there briefly before the countdown to jump. It's the moment in archery when you pull back the bow, take a deep breath, and adjust your sightline on the target before propelling the arrow forward. It's how cats of prey take a step back and pause just before attacking. It's the way butterflies rest for a moment after emerging from the cocoon before taking flight.

In order for your vision to move from energy to physical, a slight slowing-down process must occur. It's simple physics. Things that exist in the Physical World vibrate slower than those existing in energy alone. This paused moment is simply a slowing down of energy so it can manifest into the Physical World.

You may remember turning gas into liquid or liquid into solid in your high school physics class. In order for this process to happen, the vibration of electrons and protons must slow down. Take condensation for instance. When the super-fast-moving molecules of water vapor come into contact with a cool temperature, the water vapor molecules slow down. When they slow down enough, their molecular attractions overcome their speed, and they stay together as liquid water.

Your vision has massive momentum leading up to this point with loads of energy moving behind the scenes. But it must slow down to a crawl for everything to be birthed into the Physical World.

I experience this stage as an intense physical pressure that I feel in, around, and all over my body. It feels as if I'm being squeezed from every direction or I'm being pulled through a wormhole two sizes too small.

My natural, unconscious propensity during this process is to get agitated and anxious, even though I consciously know what's happening. I know the process. I know it's only through presence and breathing I find peace with the experience. Yet sometimes I can't help but succumb to the pressure.

The day before I left Los Angeles to write this book, the pressure was so intense. I woke up as usual at 6:00 a.m. to feed the cats, except Alliver wasn't eating or using the litter box. My mind jumped instantaneously to the day I returned from Bali to find that my little fur monster had been urinating blood, which then spiraled into an emergency vet visit and subsequent surgery, and kept spiraling into the six weeks of recovery—making sure she didn't pull her stitches out and was eating, while keeping her drugged, and locked her in my bathroom. Then, as if that wasn't enough, my brain moved past all the things that could go wrong with her health while I was away and into the list of possible things I was forgetting, my pending manuscript, how filthy my apartment was, the chaos I was leaving for my house sitter, and more.

I lost it. My breathing grew heavy and fast. The tears began to flow. My shoulders caved forward and my nose started to drip. For five solid hours I sat on my hot-pink couch and flowed between ugly cries and slight weeping.

In a momentary respite from my emotions, I took to Facebook to document the experience.

Just a short 24 hours until I leave LA for three weeks to write my book... and I'm officially feeling all the feels.

The tears have not stopped flowing since I got out of bed. Some a mere trickle, others eliciting full-body sobs and a snotty nose, and others failing to come out at all leaving me with a knot in my throat.

I'm scared to leave because of Alliver and her health issues that happened when I got back from Bali. She could have died. I'm scared it will happen again and I won't be here to take care of her. I'm scared that I'm a bad cat mom for leaving.

I'm scared that the book isn't going to come out right. I'm scared that I'm going to get in the way of what is asking to come through me. I'm scared that I'm not going to time manage well and won't come back to LA with a finished first draft.

I'm scared that everything is going to fall apart while I'm gone. And that it's going to take me the rest of the year to pick up the pieces like when I got back from Bali.

Despite all this fear that is circling and enveloping me this morning - I am unwilling to NOT go. I've already committed to this leap, and turning back is just not an option.

And as much as I'd like all the answers right now, that's clearly not how this is playing out (I even called a friend and asked HER to give me all the answers this morning... no such luck!).

I'm in the midst of the free-fall part of this leap. And all I can do is trust. Trust that Alliver is safe and healthy. Trust that everything is in divine perfection. Trust that the book coming through me as needed. Trust that I'm taken care of.

This is always one of the hardest parts. There's nothing to hold on to. Nothing to lean on. No points of reference or markers to calibrate my bearings as I fall.

Just the rush of air as I tumble closer and closer to the ground... praying that the parachute opens or that I can see the net (preferably sooner than later).

Authorship, here I come.

I was in the pause; the awkward space between not my leap and my leap, a slight period of nothingness before it turned into everything. And it was not graceful in any way. But my commitment was unwavering—not writing this book was not an option, so I might as well be vulnerable and transparent about the experience!

I wasn't done yet though. After this, it got even less graceful. The following day I sat on the bathroom floor, cuddling Alliver and crying for an hour. My house sitter arrived to find me a complete mess, a cocktail of scattered and emotional with a slight hint of delusion. She soothed me again and again as she ushered me out the door and into the waiting Lyft.

I got onto the airplane with a sigh of relief. Whew. I made it through to the other side.

Well, maybe that was a bit preemptive.

Again the next morning, I woke up in a puddle of tears. (That's three days in a row, in case you're keeping track.) The cat sitter hadn't messaged me yet that morning. Alliver had died. It had to be true. There could be no other reason she didn't message me. My hour drive to the hair salon was consumed with imaginary scenarios of how the conversation would go and what my response would be. Shit got dark.

I was mentally organizing how I would get back to Los Angeles to have her put down, and then turn around and return to house-sitting the same day to make sure I was back in time to feed the cats I was responsible for. I was rehearsing how I would say goodbye to her … and mapping out where I would spread her ashes.

I spun and spun myself into more tears on that drive until a little voice popped into my head: *You're being unreasonable. Take a breath. You don't know anything about what's happening at home, and you can't do a damn thing about it until you do know. Even then, you're a thousand miles away. Stop devoting your energy to this. Enjoy your drive. You're here to write. Be here.*

Being a human is such an interesting thing. Here we are, experiencing a process that is normal and natural, yet because of our consciousness we spin it into all these ridiculous (and crazy, I might add) stories and scenarios. We allow it to mean something about ourselves. So much judgment ensues.

I often wonder what would happen if caterpillars had our level of consciousness. I feel like it would go something like this:

I'm spinning this cocoon all wrong. What if it doesn't come out perfectly and the other caterpillars make fun of me? Ugh, look at Bobby's cocoon over there. It's so much better than mine is. I'm so bad at this. I should just quit.

Followed by:

Oh my. Everything is dissolving. I'm turning into liquid. Is this supposed to happen? Maybe I should turn back. This metamorphosis thing seems pretty overrated. I need to bust out of this cocoon. Get me out! I'm not committed anymore. I quit.

Followed by:

Cell division is painful. Why me? I just wanted to be a butterfly. Why do I have to go through all of this? It hurts. Cindy made it look so easy. Why was it easy for her and I have to experience all of this pain?

Followed by:

What's going on? Everything has stopped. This must be the part where I die. It's over. I'm never going to make it out to fly in the fresh breeze. I'll take one last breath. It's done. I'm dead. Oh, wait. Something just happened—I felt a crack. This chrysalis just broke open. Let me see if I can open it more.

After that little voice, I was able to gain some perspective. My mind shifted almost immediately. It was true. There wasn't anything I could do about Alliver's health. Worrying and crying weren't helping anyone, especially not myself. I made a decision in that moment: It was time to be present for my writing. I refused to devote energy to scenarios I made up in my head. From that moment forward, I would focus on being completely present, feeling the support from the Spiritual World, and funneling all my heart into this manuscript.

That shift from discomfort into action embodies this stage of the leap.

MOVING FROM PLANNING TO ACTION

The truth is you could sit around and plan your leap forever. The buildup to this point is crucial, but if you let it take over and prevent you from actually leaping, it is worthless. You can talk about it, hear about other people's experiences, read books and learn about it, all without ever doing anything about it. Your knowledge is only as powerful as your execution.

Just as you experienced the pain of being out of alignment before, you will this time as well. But now, the misalignment will be that you've gotten so far into alignment with your dreams you can't not take action on them.

> "And the day came when the risk to remain
> tight in a bud was more painful than the
> risk it took to blossom."
> - Anaïs Nin

You will experience a culmination or tipping point, which is the moment you must take action to create your vision. And I'm not saying you will be forced to take action; I'm saying you'll be unable to not take action.

This may come to you on a mental, physical, or emotional level, or a combination of them. Sometimes it will be a super-clear, definitive moment in time coming straight from the Physical World, such as getting fired from a job, the ending of a relationship, the death of a loved one, a major medical issue, etc. Sometimes it shows up as a quiet whisper or tap on your shoulder. And sometimes it shows up as a super-deep, emotional knowing.

The point is, when you get this message, you will know. There's no waiting. There are no decisions to be made. The time has arrived. Things will not look perfect. You won't have all your plans laid out. You won't feel like you're ready.

The energy and momentum has been building. It's time to do something about it. Harness all the energy you've been using to prepare, and funnel it into action, into the moment your vision is birthed into the physical world.

Your brain may tell you x, y, and z need to be in place first, but don't let it fool you. Wallace Wattles, author of *The Science of Getting Rich*, explains this conundrum perfectly: "You can so act upon the environment in which you are now, as to cause yourself to be transferred to a better environment. Hold with faith and purpose the vision of yourself in the better environment, but act upon your present environment with all your heart, and with all your strength, and with all your mind."

When your time to leap calls to you, it's crucial to act upon it from exactly where you are. A new client comes to you but you don't have your systems or website set up yet? Say "yes" anyway. You get invited to a networking event but don't have business cards yet? Go anyway.

I recently spoke with television host AJ Gibson about the catalyst moment that turned his dreams into a reality. He shared his first experience not only walking a red carpet as talent at the Billboard Music Awards in 2016, but also his first time hosting a major red carpet for Dick Clark Productions.

As each person in front of him took the carpet, he noticed their press team walking before them holding a sign with their name on it. The photographers would take a photo of the talent's name before snapping images of the person on the red carpet so they would have record of who was in each photo.

Because it was his first red carpet, AJ had no idea this was a thing. He didn't have a sign. He didn't have a press team. He was about to walk the red carpet, and not a single photographer was going to know who he was. AJ had a choice in this moment: get out of line and skip the red carpet or walk the red carpet without any photographers knowing who he was.

The funny thing is that [my co-host] didn't actually need the sign, but I knew that I certainly did! I had always shied away from the self-promotion part of the industry because the small-town Ohio boy in me never felt comfortable with it and never felt that I deserved to be there in the first place. It's almost like I knew that if the press found out who I was, they would also realize that I was a fraud and unworthy of their attention.

Despite his fears, AJ found a third option to enable him to act upon his environment in the moment. He pulled a production assistant from his duties and asked he bring him a piece of paper and marker. AJ quickly wrote his name on it and convinced the assistant to hold the sign up before him as he walked the red carpet so members of the press would know who he was.

And it worked. Just a few hours later, he was receiving message after message from people who saw him featured on Esquire magazine's Best Dressed List alongside the likes of Ludacris, Nick Jonas, and Wiz Khalifa.

The moment I received that first notification was surreal and actually seeing Getty images of myself on the red carpet was even more strange, but not because of the reasons you might think. I could give two shits about walking a red carpet or appearing on a best-dressed list, but what I did care about was the perception attached to those images. I bought my own tux, styled myself and rocked that carpet, even though I was terrified on the inside. But I also felt oddly at home on that carpet, almost like for the first time in my life, after thirty-six years, I felt that I belonged. I'd had some success up to that point, but had never fully allowed myself to accept that I had earned a seat at the table until I saw my name and—more importantly—my picture next to artists whom I admire. Needless to say, I'm glad I trusted my gut that day. Also, I've never had to make a sign since!

The lesson? Find a way to take action in your current environment so it transfers you to the one you desire. And do it now.

I prefer to treat this stage like removing a Band-Aid: rip it off quickly because the longer you let it linger, the more it hurts! I've been told it's the same with skydiving. Did you know they always count to three, but leap on two? On three, everyone grabs at the plane with death grips to prevent the leap.

Take action and never look back.

What's that saying, "Only look back to see how far you've come"? I think that's especially true when it comes to leaps. I mean, you've made it this far … why would you get back on the fence now?

Take action and never look back.

BURNING THE PROVERBIAL BOAT

That said, I have found there are two different kinds of people when it comes to leaps: the ones who burn the boat and eliminate all possible escape routes, and those who need an emergency evacuation plan just in case.

The first are the ones who burn the ship entirely so only ashes remain. Or they walk the tight rope without a safety net to catch them if they fall. This is how I operate.

I've found the more I keep my options open or maintain a safety net, the more likely I am to quit and turn back mid-leap. If I have an out, I will almost always choose it. In a choice between getting uncomfortable and staying comfortable, the human brain will always choose comfort.

If I remove the choice for comfort, my hand is forced and I have to choose discomfort. My business has excelled more in the moments when I have nothing else to lean back on. My life has expanded more in the moments when I don't have an opt-out because if the ship is gone, I can't turn back, and if there is no net under the tightrope, falling is not an option.

When I was moving to LA, an acquaintance casually closed our conversation with, "Good luck with the move. I mean, you can always move back to Washington!" What I wouldn't give now to have a photo of my reaction to this comment. I responded, "Oh no, that's not an option," before politely ending the conversation and walking away.

Because I removed the option of moving back to Washington, I knew I would be forced to make Los Angeles work for me. If I had even a whisper of, "I can move back," pop up in my mind every time things got hard, there would be no way I'd be approaching my fifth anniversary in Los Angeles. I would have moved back ages ago.

And while this idea of burning the ship (along with all the emergency rowboats!) or removing the safety nets works for me, it doesn't work for everyone. The second type of people are those who need to keep an energetic emergency rowboat or a safety net because the idea of leaping without it paralyzes them.

I was talking about this concept with my dear friend Adrienne Pieroth. While I am the person who would energetically be "The Man on the Wire"—no safety net with everything on the line crossing between the Twin Towers—she needs a safety net. Removing all other options motivates me and pushes me further than if I have an option to NOT put myself out there. Adrienne is the exact opposite.

Everybody says to "burn the boat." So here I am, leaping with the idea that I should burn the boats, but the reality is when I try to do it that way, I experience complete paralysis. It stops me in my tracks. I feel like I'm a trapped animal. Yes, I've leapt to this island to follow my vision, but all I can focus on are the burned boats and I become paralyzed.

I don't want to call it an "out" because once I leap I've leapt. But knowing the worst-case scenarios and identifying what I could fall back on if necessary propels me forward into my vision even more than completely being without other options. I'm the kind of person who needs some kind of grounding. A connection root to tether me to something real. Put me anywhere, but as long as I can feel the stability of putting a root down I'll be fine. If I don't have that, I feel like I'm floating around. That level of uncertainty doesn't work for me.

For Adrienne, burning the boats puts her too far out of her comfort zone. It pushes her out into the danger zone, yet it puts me in my premium zone for productivity and momentum. What may be my level of motivation could trigger your five-alarm fire signal forcing you to evacuate.

Know yourself and what you need. Are you someone who needs to remove all other options in order to feel motivated to leap? Or does the idea of removing all the safety nets prevent you from taking action? Look back on some leaps you've taken in the past. What helped you move forward with your leap? Was it removing all the safety nets or keeping one to prevent paralysis? What worked in your past leaps and what didn't work?

Learning from what has and hasn't worked for you before can support you in feeling safer and help you move forward.

Be honest with yourself. This level of self-awareness will only support you in creating your desired outcome. What do you need to be successful in your leap?

Why is it that some people operate at this level of do-or-die and others require something to fall back on in order to move forward? It's a combination of nature and nurture. Medical studies have actually begun to understand our bodies and brains process stress differently.

Take for example Alex Honnold, the guy who free-climbed El Capitan in Yosemite National Park—without a rope. In March 2016, Honnold went to the Medical University of South Carolina in Charleston to undergo a functional magnetic resonance imaging (fMRI) brain scan (MacKinnon 2016). This machine detects activity in the various regions of the brain by tracing blood flow. Cognitive neuroscientist Jane Joseph volunteered to execute the scan.

Of particular interest was Honnold's amygdala, the main area of the brain that processes and interprets our threat responses. It receives information from our senses and dictates our behavior and triggers our fight-or-flight response. The amygdala also sends information through the structures of the brain, where it may be translated into the conscious emotion of fear.

Joseph had a theory Honnold was missing an amygdala completely; however, the scan showed otherwise. While completing the scan, Honnold was shown widely used imagery meant to evoke strong emotional responses by disturbing or exciting the patient. These images are meant to trigger the amygdala, yet he was having no response.

Joseph was completely unable to spot any activity anywhere in the fear center of Honnold's brain. The conclusion was that Honnold really does have an extraordinary brain, one that does not process fear in the ways that most brains do. "Where there is no activation," she says, "there probably is no threat response."

Neuroscientist Joseph LeDoux performed a secondary anaysis. "[Honnold's] brain is probably predisposed to be less reactive to threats that other people would be naturally responsive to, simply because of the choices he's made," LeDoux says. "On top of that, these self-imposed strategies that he's using make that even better, or stronger."

Honnold is clearly an extreme example of the brain's nature to uniquely process stress and fear that would put him into the "burn the boat" category.

Additionally, my friend Adrienne recently learned through testing that her inability to burn the boats may be due to a genetic variant. Because she possesses the MTHFR C677T mutation, she does not process stress the same way the average person does. Genetically she is 30 percent less efficient at processing stress physiologically than an average person, which helps explain why it's scarier for her to leap into uncertainty without some sort of safety net.

And, of course, nurture plays into this conversation as well. The way in which we are raised, as well as the societal expectations and conditioning we subscribe to, directly impacts how we leap.

Being raised by a parent who is highly risk-averse can impact your view on changes in life, as well as your ability to manage and execute leaps. Children who are constantly sheltered and prevented from experiencing and learning how to navigate uncertainty will be less likely to develop the muscles needed to leap without a net. Growing up in a society or culture that encourages you to follow the well-worn path will engrain that path as the only option discouraging you from deviating from it.

Take this opportunity to learn about your beliefs from your upbringing, determine how you best process stress, and do the work to know whether or not you need to burn the boat.

Here are some questions to get you started:

1. What are the things you think of when you are considering a risky decision?

2. What does it feel like to remove all options but your leap? Does it feel empowering or paralyzing?

3. What does it feel like to keep a few options in your life in case your leap doesn't work out? Does it feel safer for you to pursue your leap, or does it feel more like a lazy approach that would prevent you from putting your full effort forth?

4. How do you process stress in your life?

5. What motivates you—being backed up against a wall with no choice but to be successful, or having the space to breathe and create with no pressing external stimulus?

Dive into these questions and more when you access the resources at http://permissiontoleap.today.

HOW TO COMBAT THE FEELING OF BEING OVERWHELMED

Whatever you decide about your boats and your nets, the actual leap can be incredibly overwhelming. I interviewed several people about skydiving experiences in preparation for writing this book, and my main question was how they fared during the free fall—the moments between the jump and the landing. All of them echoed one very important technique: massive presence.

Why is this? Fear, anxiety, stress, and the feeling of being overwhelmed do not live in the present moment. These emotions are a result of your past life experiences or a result of future pacing an anticipated event that has not yet happened and may never happen (or a combination of the two!). We fall back into replaying the results of our past experiences, we "what if" ourselves to death, or we apply our past results to our futures.

Once we are present with this moment though, and ask ourselves, "what is true for me right now in this exact moment?" we can often remove the fear, anxiety, and stress we experience with our leap. Constantly looking at the totality of the leap can induce paralysis.

I want to ask you a question. It's a bit weird, but it's one of my favorites.

How do you eat an elephant?

Any guesses? Thoughts?

I'll tell you: one bite at a time.

Your leap is not a gigantic, one-time event. There will likely be some sort of occasion to mark the actual leap: writing the book, launching the website, signing your first client, getting married, selling everything you own, moving to a new place, etc. But it will end up being a series of daily decisions strung together to create momentum and your vision day by day.

Looking at the entirety of the picture can spin you into taking no action because there are too many actions to take. Get present, connect with the Spiritual World for guidance, and slow down.

I spoke about this with Sheila Viers on the *Permission to Leap* podcast. Sheila explained how she focused on the individual steps, rather than the entire, full vision. "I knew the next step of what I could do. That was how all my leaps came together. I always talk about it's as if you're crossing a river on stepping-stones. You step on the first, then you take a step to the next stepping-stone, then the next. With each passing stone, you have a totally different perspective, and you see different opportunities because you've grown. It's almost like you don't know what the path is going to look like because all you have prior to that is experience from the past, which is such a limited perspective. You don't know you don't know until you know it. You can never really know the whole way there. So you take one step at a time."

Take it day by day, allowing the next actions to reveal themselves. I prefer to use the space created during my daily practice to receive inspiration from the Spiritual World to guide and direct me in my daily life.

During this time, I like to ask, "What can I do today, exactly where I am, using the resources that I currently possess, in order to create [insert vision here]?" This question shifts the perspective from victimhood and feeling overwhelmed to one of presence and empowerment. It will give you smaller, bite-sized action items to follow through with on a daily basis.

Addressing the question on a regular basis helps you ensure the answers you're receiving are from an aligned place, rather than your mind jumping in to force the next steps or taking steps that were aligned with the beginning of your journey, but are out of alignment with where you are now.

Because it's not just about taking action. Anyone can get up and take action every day. Instead, it's about taking *aligned* action. It's about using the energy from the Spiritual World to support you in determining your actions in the Physical World. It is this combination of the Physical World and the Spiritual World that creates an exponential spike in your results.

It is these small, incremental steps and actions in the present moment that add up and build to "critical mass" for your end vision to not only be created in the world, but also sustained. And it is a consistent application of concentration, courage, and patience that will determine your success.

Remember, it's better to allow your actions to be revealed to you. Pushing, forcing, or otherwise manipulating your actions will only produce results aligned with that energy. It used to be a badge of honor to create in this way; however, this is no longer the case. Using inspiration from the Spiritual World to create in the Physical World will always produce the results most highly aligned with your vision.

Another great way to bring your energy into the present moment is through grounding, the practice of centering yourself within your body and connecting it to the energy of the Earth. The easiest way to do this is to put your bare feet on the Earth—sitting in the grass with the soles of your feet on the ground, walking along the shore, etc.

You can also use a grounding meditation to envision your energy mixing with the energy of the Spiritual World, and then extending it through the soles of your feet to sink into the Earth. I've recorded my favorite grounding meditation, which you can access at http://permissiontoleap. today.

Relying on this connection will support you in remaining present, as well as releasing any anxiety, tension, or stress you are experiencing. Plus, it reinforces the divine intersection of heaven and Earth!

10. Create Your Feedback Loop

You have taken the leap. Now what?

This is the stage where you get the opportunity to consistently apply the tools you have learned in order to maintain momentum and upswing. Your leap will be marked by a thing or moment in time, but unlike skydiving, building a vision requires a long-term commitment.

CONTINUE THE MOMENTUM

In order to ensure you are maintaining this alignment moving forward, create a system for checking in with yourself and your leap. It should be a system to look at the past, present, and future and identify what is working, as well as what isn't working. Without this, you may start down a path that isn't working without realizing it until it's too late.

A successful feedback loop will be a systematic method you use to intentionally maximize learning, minimize wrong turns, and guide you down your best path. In order to ensure you are maintaining this alignment moving forward, I'm going to show you exactly how to create your own feedback loop.

Psychologist Albert Bandura studied the psychology behind why this works. His studies of children revealed that giving them a goal coupled with a specific evaluation process greatly increased the likelihood of their success. Conversely, the children with a specific goal but no evaluation process were less likely to successfully achieve their goal.

I found this to be especially true with my first business. My relocation from Olympia to Los Angeles was primarily fueled by my eponymous fashion brand. I landed in LA and hit the ground running. I ran and I ran and I ran. But at some point, I lost my focus on what I was running toward and never stopped to evaluate the direction I was moving in.

Day after day, I kept going without looking up and without pausing. I was working myself to the bone with nothing to show for it. Returning home every evening felt like a respite from having run a marathon on a hamster wheel all day. I was expending all this energy and had nothing to show for it. I was exhausted, and my creativity was zapped.

How had I gotten so far away from the alignment I had when I created this brand? I didn't implement a consistent daily practice, I lost my connection to my vision, and I never paused to assess where I was. At some point along the line, I took a turn unaligned with my vision, but because I wasn't connected to my vision, I had no idea it happened, and I continued to move forward.

By the time I realized what happened, it was too late. I had journeyed so far away from my initial intention and vision for the brand there was no going back. Here was a dream I had been building since I was little. My heart was so connected to this business inspired by my grandmother. My ego was so connected to the illusion of being a fashion designer, and yet I hadn't been capable of remaining connected to it.

Instead of being in the present joy and creativity of it, the constant story in my head was questioning how the financial aspect of the business would play out. Instead of visualizing and aligning in the present moment, I constantly pushed away success by remaining in the energy of how things weren't working. Instead of doing something about what wasn't working, I put my power in the hands of others and blamed the industry, buyers, influencers, etc.

Looking back now, I see so many ways that could have transformed everything about my ability to create the fashion brand I envisioned. But instead, I reached a point of no return leaving me no option but to walk away and close my doors.

"I think it's very important to have a feedback loop, where you're constantly thinking about what you've done and how you could be doing it better. I think that's the single best piece of advice: constantly think about how you could be doing things better and questioning yourself."
Elon Musk

Continuously assessing your progress will mitigate your risk and accelerate your results. It forces you to be honest about what activities are bridging the gap between your present and your future, as well as which ones are widening it. And, once you're aware, you have the opportunity to stop doing the things that are not working while doubling down on the things that are.

You can begin this process by looking at what your end goal is, and make two lists: what is currently bringing you closer to this goal, and what is pulling you farther away from this goal?

One thing to be aware of is it's not enough to simply observe the answers to these questions; you also need to address how knowing this information will change your actions, thoughts, and behaviors to keep you moving in the direction of your vision. Gathering feedback is just the beginning. It's the interpretation and implementation that are crucial.

Implementing what you've learned during this process can literally change everything. Adjusting your attitude, behavior, and actions to align with what's working is what differentiates mediocre from excellence.

IMPLEMENT A FEEDBACK LOOP

As simple as this sounds, most people struggle with the implementation of the feedback loop. Looking at our behaviors, actions, and thoughts on a consistent basis can feel cumbersome. The best way to implement this is to plan out a systematic approach to address these important questions on a regular basis.

The basic flow of a feedback loop consists of taking the initial action, interpreting the results of that action, and then determining your next steps.

When you take the action to move onto your first stepping-stone, pause before moving to the next stone and ask yourself: What results did that action produce? Was that result beneficial, and did it create the kind of impact I want?

Systems like this can not only give you information about your current actions and results, but the consistent attention on what you are creating will also support you in making choices more aligned with your goals and vision.

I have found weekly or biweekly feedback is the most beneficial. If too much time passes between check-in points, you are more likely to diverge from your path. Schedule and plan a period of time each week to evaluate and reassess what's working and what isn't working to move forward with alignment.

Here are some examples of feedback loops that could spark ideas for your own process:

- If you want to increase your financial abundance, set up a weekly money date. Schedule thirty minutes a week into your calendar to track what money you are spending, what money you are investing, and what money you are earning, and do your tax planning. Identify where you are on budget, where you are over- or underspending, and how you will change your spending habits from here forward.

- If you're looking to strengthen your relationships, schedule a weekly check-in with your partner (this works for business or personal relationships). Schedule a non-negotiable connection time to talk about your relationship, how each of you is feeling, what's working and not working in the relationship, and how each of you needs to be supported.

- If you're looking to improve your physical health, utilize a health-tracking app or movement monitoring device to collect data for you, and set up a time every week to look back at your achievements, as well as look forward toward your upcoming goals.

- If you're looking to improve your diet, set up a weekly time for grocery planning and implementation. Then look over your health habits from the past week to determine when you felt your best, when you didn't feel your best, what choices were associated with each of those feelings, and what needs to be different moving forward to increase your "feel best" state.

- If you're dating, create a practice of checking in with yourself after each date. Identify what you liked about the experience, what was important to you during the date, what you preferred to be different, and what you would like to experience the next time.

I have condensed my feedback loop system into a worksheet to assist you with the process. Visit http://permissiontoleap.today to download a copy and begin using it today!

REFINE YOUR FOCUS, INCREASE YOUR IMPACT

It's best to employ focus as you're creating your vision. You can take a million actions all day long, but—not only do you not have time for that—when you spread your focus across a million actions, you diminish the impact they have. So why not focus on the actions working for you and leave behind the actions not creating the results you desire? The more energy you funnel into what's working, the more power you can generate to increase your results.

Take the sun as an example. When the sun is diffused over half the surface of the earth, it creates light and warmth but doesn't make a significant impact. But when you can funnel the energy of the sun into a single ray through a magnifying glass, it will start a fire.

The feedback loop will help you not only differentiate between what's working and what's not working, it will focus your actions and energy on only what is working to produce results. If you do this, there will be no choice but to start a fire.

And how will you know that you're starting a fire? Well, you'll continually perform this feedback process and have demonstrated results you can review to tell you how it's working.

For example, say you have an online business. In this online business you are using Facebook, Twitter, Instagram, LinkedIn, email campaigns, YouTube, etc. to market yourself. You're only able to put a minimal effort into each of these areas and are dividing the time you spend working by all six platforms. You are diffusing your energy.

Then you begin to implement this feedback loop and learn only two of those platforms are actually bringing you new clients and generating revenue. Would you continue putting your focus on the four areas not creating an impact, or would you funnel all your energy into the two areas that work and leave the rest?

You could stay in the overwhelming busy-ness of it all or, through regular assessment, you could become aware of where to divert your energy to make the biggest impact in your business and the lives of your clients.

When I transitioned out of fashion and into my coaching business, I began a regular practice of checking in with my business. Each week I sit down to assess what worked that week, what did not work, what felt good, and what I would be willing to let go of or do differently in order to create my vision. Since there is no predetermined road map for being an entrepreneur, it's especially important to check your trajectory regularly. Otherwise you end up way off the path, like I did with my fashion brand, with little chance of getting back on track.

While it's really easy to see how this concept works for entrepreneurship, be aware it works for all leaps—relationships, careers, parenting, happiness, mindset, health, finances, etc. It's a simple process of initial action, information, and response.

In relationships, asking questions of yourself or your partner such as, "How could I have been a better partner this week?" or "What made you feel most supported in our relationship this week?" can give you the information you need to adjust your actions and create different results.

For your health, asking, "How did I feel in my body this week? What did I do that felt amazing? What did I do that didn't feel so great? What did I consume to help my body function better—or what makes my body function worse?" will provide you with data indicating what works and what doesn't so you can then change your actions.

For your mindset, asking, "What beliefs supported me this week? What thoughts, beliefs, or attitudes are hindering my ability to be successful?" will reveal to you where you are hitting your own glass ceiling, thus allowing you to alter things so as to surpass your limits.

Remember, any information gained during your feedback loop is just that—information. There is no need to be ashamed of any decisions, actions, etc. in which you have engaged in the past. There's no going back to change what has happened—just the ability to course correct for the future. There's no need to go down the spiral of feeling worse and worse. Simply look at the data as objectively as possible and determine whether you are committed to changing your thoughts, behaviors, and/or actions. Possessing this data and knowledge is what aligns your behavior with your desired outcome.

When you identify a particular activity or action that isn't working, you need to be incredibly honest with yourself. Are you committed to eliminating that particular thing from your behaviors? Sometimes the answer will be a clear "yes," and you will have no hesitation letting it go. Other times it won't be so cut and dry. If you're unable to have a definitive "I will not do this again," don't be hard on yourself; instead, set a deadline, which will enable you to gather more data about the action and evaluate the results on several occasions.

After analyzing this broad range of information, you can decide if you are committed to giving up the behavior or not. If you decide to give up the behavior, you will refine your focus and increase the power being directed at your vision. If you decide not to give up the behavior, you will continue to diffuse your energy and lessen your impact on creating your vision. At the end of the day, the decision is up to you.

LEAPING IS A MARATHON, NOT A SPRINT

I can't stress the importance of your inner foundation enough. This is when the work really begins.

Hustle mode becomes incredibly seductive. Our vision narrows and building our dreams becomes all-consuming, which means we let our practices fall to the wayside. It's incredibly common to stop checking in with your soul, drop your routines and habits, and spiral back into focusing only on the Physical World.

This is when I hear, "I don't have time for myself. My vision is everything. It takes priority. I have too much to do and I'm not doing enough." By failing to prioritize yourself and your connection to the Spiritual World, you are failing yourself and your dream. Busy-ness will get you nowhere. Intentional, creative focus will get you everywhere.

Life will always continue to ebb and flow, expand and contract. It's the natural rhythm of life—but it's never about the rhythm. It's about how you respond to it.

A mentor once pointed out the parallel between this natural rhythm and a heart monitor. You know a person is alive because of the peaks and valleys. A flat line means death.

There will always be ups and downs in life. It means you're alive. So it's not about the movement of living; it's about having the resiliency to manage it, and this resiliency comes from the Spiritual World, not the Physical World.

There will always be things fighting against you. This path is not for people looking to live an "easy" existence. Yes, you can breathe ease into the experience of creating your vision, but it's not a one-time thing. You must show up for your vision and your leap every day.

I had a conversation with a girlfriend while writing this wherein she said, "But, Bri, it's hard!" Yeah, it is. It is possible for your vision to materialize quickly, but it doesn't mean it's going to be without bumps, roadblocks, and detours. The trick is to not allow these bumps, roadblocks, and detours to derail you—to stay in alignment with your vision, remain connected to your leap, and use your inner foundation to support you in continuing to move forward despite perceived setbacks.

Use the tools and resources in this book to build your inner foundation. The resiliency will come from maintaining this inner foundation day in and day out. Focus on your "why," and spend time in your heart and your vision. Check in with your future self. Practice gratitude. Connect to the Spiritual World. Take aligned action.

You didn't read this book just to gather information. This is where your commitment at the beginning of being a Creator will be tested. How will you show up for your vision every day, now that the wheels are in motion? Who will you become in order to support the continued unfolding and expansion of your vision in the world?

Use the exercises within this book again and again to continue to strengthen your foundation as you move forward with your vision into the world. This process is not a "one-and-done" methodology. Revisit the phases of the leap and associated tools because a leap requires you to show up every day. Use this book and the resources located at http://permissiontoleap.today to continually remind you how.

CONTINUALLY STRENGTHEN YOUR INNER FOUNDATION

You now have an opportunity to allow your daily conscious choice to transform into your life through regular, repeated application. At some point, you won't need to wake up and consciously choose your leap; it will become your way of life. It will become who you are. It's when you stop effort-ing yourself into alignment and just LIVE your alignment.

Where your brain was categorizing this as dangerous just months prior, it has now become your new normal. Your leap created massive upswing and growth, and now it's about maintenance and continuing to build steadily.

Applying the Stages of Competence is incredibly helpful when looking at building your internal design to truly live your alignment.

Over the course of this book, you've gained the tools you need to create your vision. Before picking up this book, these were things that you weren't utilizing and maybe didn't even know existed. This is the first stage of competence: You didn't know what you didn't know. You had an inkling something more was available to you, but you didn't have the perspective to understand it.

Then you transcended that stage by picking up this book, and you moved into the second stage of competence: you know that you don't know something, but now what? You've opened up to what "more" could be and have said "yes" to it. You connected with your vision, but did not have the full knowledge of what would be required for it to be created in the world. You recognized you had a deficit in understanding how to move forward, which got you here, reading this very page in this very moment.

Throughout reading this, you moved into the third stage of competence by beginning to understand the steps, focus, and application needed. You have gained the knowledge and awareness to realize what is required to birth your dreams into the Physical World. You've likely begun to practice with the tools contained in these pages, and now you get to apply these day in and day out because in order to continue the forward momentum, you must keep practicing and applying.

During this third stage, your practice requires a high level of concentration. You still have to consciously apply effort in order to execute. You must choose your practice day in and day out. You are forging those pathways in your brain, but it requires you to consistently make a conscious decision.

And finally, the fourth stage of competence comes once you have applied continuous conscious effort long enough it becomes an unconscious habit. You have worn down the pathway in your brain enough that a conscious decision is no longer necessary. The behavior has become second nature and no longer requires concentration. Your practice has turned into a habit, just like I explained in Chapter 5.

It's prior to this final step that most people give up. This is the part where it gets hard, people become impatient, and they fall back to their old brain pathways to determine their behavior. It's been commonly understood it takes twenty-one days of consistent application to make something a habit, but scientific research over the last decade has shown otherwise.

Phillippa Lally published her study on habit formation in 2009, in which she studied ninety-six participants to observe the length of time required to turn a conscious activity into an automatic action. The study revealed it took the participants from eighteen to 254 days for this process to occur, with an average of sixty-six days, and of the habits the participants chose, drinking a glass of water took less time to establish as a habit than developing an exercise routine.

What does this mean for you? It means this is a process that will likely require your attention and focus beyond the standard twenty-one-day habit-creation time frame. The creation process requires work and commitment. The content and tools in this book will not work for you unless you work for them.

Do yourself a favor and set yourself up for success. Put together a routine or a system to support you in implementing what you've learned and stick to it. Reread this book and interact with your vision by following the worksheets until the tools become second nature. Schedule weekly time to complete your feedback loop. Use the psychology of accountability to support you in building a community or investing in a coach to ensure that you make it over the finish line.

Yes, there are going to be things outside your control that will affect the creation of your vision. You have to do what you can with what you have to ensure it doesn't derail you … because the likelihood of being derailed during this process is very, very high. But here's the cool part: it's not about the derailment. It's about how you respond to it and what you do on the other side of being derailed.

If you notice yourself getting off track through the course of one of your regular feedback loop check-ins, give yourself some space to inquire about the cause of misalignment. Sitting in silence and curiosity can help you gain the awareness of why you have been derailed from your vision, and then you can do the work to get back into alignment.

There will always be situations and circumstances distracting you from your vision. Always. Without exception. And you will likely get pulled into them. It's up to you to catch yourself when it happens and bring yourself back on track.

Build your habits to support your success. Gather people around you who are holding you accountable (have you joined the *Permission to Leap* community on Facebook yet?). Remove the choices to not show up for your vision. Give your vision everything you have. Focus your energy. Show up every damn day.

And on the days when you feel like you can't, because there will be days like this, reach out to someone. Get support. Give yourself a moment to lose your shit. Love on yourself with massive compassion.

Then get back to building your vision. Remember: the world needs you.

One of the best ways I have found to keep my focus on my vision is to write a personal declarative statement (otherwise known as a mission statement) to be used to guide your thoughts and beliefs, consistently reminding you of why you chose to leap in the first place. You can hang this statement around your home or office, incorporate it into your feel-ization, and create laptop wallpaper. Remember, simply reading this as a mantra will not work. You must feel and embody this statement in order for it to turn into a habit and create a new brain pathway.

11. Permission to Leap

THOUGHTS ON SUCCESS AND FAILURE

Everyone wants to know their leap will be successful prior to taking it, which, as you've learned, isn't a guaranteed possibility. But what if it could be possible to know—beyond a shadow of a doubt—it would be successful?

Here's the hard thing about leaps: there is never a guarantee. Will every leap you take 100 percent match exactly how you envisioned it in your mind? Probably not. Does this mean you shouldn't do it? Absolutely not.

What if success and failure were not opposite ends of a spectrum, but instead coexisted? From my experience, these two states overlap more than you realize. What keeps our successes hidden behind our failures is our perception of the situation.

Take me for example. I've officially said goodbye to 80 percent of the projects I have birthed in the last ten years. That's a pretty high percentage, which means I've had only a 20 percent success rate for creating my visions. Do I wake up in the mornings and see an 80 percent failure rate looking back at me in the mirror? No.

Take Thomas Edison as another example. He had 1,000 unsuccessful attempts at inventing the light bulb, a .0999 percent success rate. But instead of seeing 1,000 failures, he viewed it like this: "I didn't fail 1,000 times. The light bulb was an invention with 1,000 steps." The legacy of Thomas Edison is not colored by his 1,000 failures, but instead by the journey and commitment it took for him to have one success, which was the only success he needed, and our world is forever changed because of it.

How do you remove this perceived dichotomy between success and failure? Begin to look at every leap as a part of your larger journey. There will be something to learn in every endeavor that you undertake. I recently heard an interview with the founder of Dollar Shave Club about success and failure:

"All of these projects are worthwhile because they're building my body of work. So while a specific project may not have caught fire or made a million dollars or grown into a humongous thing—someone may look at it and say, 'Wait a minute, look at this thing this guy did. Maybe we should hire him or bring him in to speak.' I view it as pieces of experience even if they don't succeed. People respect that—they'll say that's pretty cool you did this and respect to you for making it."

Success and failure are not mutually exclusive. They absolutely coexist. What if the point of you taking this leap isn't as black and white as "will it succeed or will it fail?" What if, instead, every leap was just preparing you for another leap yet to come?

The issue is you can't see the secondary leap until you have taken the first one. And you won't be able to open your energy to the next leap if you're still holding onto the failure of the last one.

I can, with absolute certainty, say I would not be writing this book or coaching women or speaking on stages if I had not gone through the experiences in my fashion brand. That business served as the training wheels for my current vision. What I learned while developing and creating that business set me so far ahead when I pivoted to create this business.

I look at the first seven years of my entrepreneurial career while in fashion as my years of being a business owner. It was a constant roller coaster of highs and lows. I was unable to hold the gigantic container I currently hold. I made a lot of mistakes. I learned more than I even knew at the time.

And because of it, I was able to graduate from being a business owner to becoming an entrepreneur. What's the difference, you may ask? As a business owner of a fashion brand, I was a designer who was responding to the daily stimuli of owning a fashion company. I wasn't leading the business (most days it was leading me!). I wasn't innovating. I wasn't being the Creator. And I wouldn't be an entrepreneur today without having experienced the difference.

So, yes, while that business technically "failed," I don't view it as a failure. I view it as a buildup leading me to where I am right now in this moment. I view it as experience and learning, as a leap that prepared me for my current leap.

Don't get me wrong—saying goodbye to a project I built is not a seamless process. But that's when I lean on my faith. I trust that if my current project is meant to be finished, it will, and conversely, if it's meant to be done, it will. Who knows—I likely won't be doing this whole writing, coaching, speaking thing for the rest of my life. And that's OK.

If that's meant to be the case, I can't force myself to remain in alignment. But that by no means is an indication I should give up on my vision, decide not to create what's in my heart, or hold myself back from putting my full effort into being present and showing up fully for what is here right now.

EXPERIENCE YOUR FULFILLMENT NOW

Our destination is always a moving target. Being in a state of constantly focusing on the success or failure of that target will leave you in a persistent state of not-enoughness. Enjoy and be present with each now-moment as you are building your future. Bridge the chasm between your now and your target with each passing moment, and be in pleasure while doing it.

If your goal is far off on the horizon and you're waiting to be happy, fulfilled, or successful until you get there, your wait will be long and painful. If you delay your happiness, fulfillment, and success until a future moment (especially the farther out it is), you won't maintain the momentum to reach your target. Without continuous positive reinforcement, you will be less likely to continue choosing your leap every day.

I can't tell you how often I hear the phrase, "When I experience x, then I will be y." For example:

- When I'm in a relationship, then I'll feel complete.

- When I have my dream job, then I'll be content at work.

- When I move into my perfect home, then I'll feel safe.

- When I make six figures, then I'll have enough money.

- When I start my business, then I'll feel fulfilled.

- When I can travel like I want, then I'll enjoy my life.

If you can't experience the feelings you are looking for in the present moment, your goal or leap will never provide it for you. Just like I talked about earlier, the feelings come first. You must find a way to experience your desired happiness, fulfillment, and success now.

Stop waiting for your Physical World to change before you step into your happiness, fulfillment, and success. It is your current experience of happiness, fulfillment, and success that allows your Physical World to change. What are some ways you can make a regular effort to exist in your "then" state now?

IT'S ALL ABOUT THE JOURNEY

In the end, it's the journey that matters the most. That's what you'll remember. Regardless of the outcome of your leap, it's the moments in the midst of creating your vision that are most important. It's the experience. It's the expansion. It's the journey.

This year, 2017, has been completely different than I anticipated. When I set out to create my year, I was simply excited to recreate what I had created the year prior, and instead, I have had the opportunity to give birth to something even more epic than I could have ever imagined from the Physical World.

My process to get off the fence was a little more than a single decision. In fact, for the first three weeks of 2017, I was trying to barter and bargain my way out of committing to my vision. During every meditation, I found myself asking, "But do I really have to say 'yes'?"

The answer day after day was the same: "Yes, yes you do."

I finally solidified my commitment in late January as I enrolled in a training program to retrain my wealth mindset. Just a few weeks later, I found myself having conversations and meetings with my accountant and financial planner about my then-nonexistent employees and seven-figure business. Around the same time is when this book made itself known to me.

I knew the Universe had heard me shortly thereafter when I began to see how out of alignment my Physical World was with my new leap. The free training that had drawn thousands of women the year prior was now attracting only a couple hundred. I received barely any interest in the ten-week group program I had been leading during all of 2016. My secondary business stopped feeling good and started feeling like a burden and an obligation.

I received an invitation to step back and examine the relationships with those closest to me. I was unable to ignore the fact that I needed to move my body more. The men I was meeting in my dating life didn't match up with who I was becoming.

When I say I let go of everything, I even had to stop watching several of my "I know they're terrible but I love them anyway" television shows.

My commitment to such a huge vision changed everything. I had no choice but to energetically clean house.

No more free training. Time to axe the group program. I quit dating. My second business and associated podcast folded. I let go of several relationships and strengthened several others. I watched the season finales of my comfort shows, knowing I'd never see them again.

I upped my healing practices (reiki, acupuncture, massage, and sound baths) for even deeper and more consistent release of my old ways. Suspended yoga became a way of life. I invested in feng shui-ing my home.

As I realigned my life, I began to increase my visualization practice again. I sat down to do a "Future-Self Meditation" and was brought to tears by what I experienced:

I found myself backstage at a theater in Seattle, listening to the sounds of hundreds of people taking their seats in the house. My body was filled with a nervous, excited energy. Butterflies danced in my stomach, a sharp tingling washed over my palms, and my heart beat so hard I thought it would explode in my chest.

I stood behind the curtain on stage right, looking out at two oversized chairs on the stage and my interviewer standing in the wings of stage left. The lights in the theater dimmed, causing the jam-packed, sold-out audience to hush.

My interviewer took the stage as lights illuminated our chairs and the audience broke out into applause. I heard her speak some words, the audience laughed, and then the stagehand was ushering me out, front and center to loud applause, a standing ovation, cheers, and all my loved ones sitting in the first several rows.

I took my seat on stage in one of the oversized chairs, noticing a table sitting in the middle with a nice array of *Permission to Leap* books on display.

The interview—actually more of a fireside chat than an interview—went by in a flash, and I found myself standing at the front of the stage thanking everyone while they all stood to thank me back.

My heart was filled with more gratitude than I ever experienced in my life. I felt tears well up in my eyes, as my throat became a little choked. This is what it was like to live your dreams and be on purpose to serve the world.

Before the meditation came to a close, I walked backstage to hug my mom, knowing I would be on my way to the lobby to sign books and meet the attendees before hitting up the after-party with my friends.

I came out of the meditation knowing this visual was so real. Part of me even realized this vision would come to life in 2018, and it is the same vision I've been playing with and living into during this leap.

Then came my Universal Double-Check moment. Throughout the year, I was speaking with a marketing company to help with my book. In January when the book came to me, we had our first conversation. But something within me knew it wasn't right, so I declined the opportunity.

In May, they reached out again to have a conversation. With just five weeks before I was to leave to write my book, I knew I needed some help, but working with them terrified me. Not only was it a huge investment, it also meant that I would have no choice but to make my vision a reality.

My cave[wo]man mind spun so many scenarios about why I should decline, how I wasn't financially in a place to commit to such a contract, and all the reasons working with them would mean sudden and imminent death.

I spent nearly the entire month of May in tears, anxious and fearful. I lost my power completely and started asking people for advice (yes, even despite rule No. 1: don't ever ask for advice). I hopped back up on the damn fence, which made me cry even more because it's so uncomfortable up there!

Then I got quiet. I looked my fears in the face to determine which were real and which were mere projections. I assessed the reality of completing this book without their support. I decided what was most important to me. And I signed the contract.

Immediately things started coming into alignment. I received more clarity about my coaching programs (because clarity is a natural by-product of commitment, alignment, and visualization!). I realized why my ten-week program was no longer in alignment and created a six-month program enabling women to go more in depth, create their leaps in real time, and receive a greater level of support during the process.

I was asking for clarity on the content of this book, and while it had been trickling in drip by drip, I was so not prepared to write it. After moving through my Universal Double-Check, the content poured into my heart, and I pulled together my book outline in an afternoon.

Then came the leap: leaving Los Angeles for my three-week writing excursion. The Band-Aid was ripped off. I was being shoved out of the proverbial plane. Kicked out of the proverbial nest. Diving off the cliff. And I was learning to fly on the way down—hoping and praying the net would appear or the parachute would open.

All I could do was focus on one day at a time. Grounding became my breathing. Massages, floating, and sound baths were my way of life. I surrounded myself with my favorite people to cheer me on.

Then one afternoon, while chatting with a good friend, it hit me: the next logical step was the Permission to Leap podcast.

At the time of writing this, I find myself in the feedback loop portion of the process. Every day I am conversing with my vision, assessing what is and isn't working, building my team, and showing up.

As much as I wish I could wrap it all up in a lovely bow for you, this is the thing: my leap is still unfolding. In your hands you hold one of the stepping-stones on my journey to create my vision.

Some days I'm confident and convinced it's happening sooner than I imagine. Some days I wake up thinking I need to be committed to an insane asylum. Some days I am inspired to work fourteen hours in pursuit of my vision, and yet others I can't even look at my business. Some days I am insanely paralyzed by fear and overwhelmed by my current reality.

I have no idea if this leap will come out as planned. I can't look into the future and definitively know if or when I will have a seven-figure business. I don't have confirmation as to whether or not this book will be a best seller or if I'll get a publisher on board to help me with distribution.

What I do know is I refuse to not show up. I know beyond a shadow of a doubt that no matter the outcome of my current leap, I said "yes" to an epic journey. I opened myself up to the joys and the pains of following my guidance and my vision.

And I always come back to trusting in the process. I personally use all the tools and resources in this book to help keep me on track. When I feel myself getting derailed, I make space to decipher and heal the underlying reasons before continuing to move forward.

Committing to a leap of faith is a crazy, beautiful process. It becomes a continuous way of life to inspire you to dream bigger, aim higher, and create more than you ever thought possible.

What I have realized is in the process of this leap (and all my previous leaps), the woman I have become this year is astonishing. The changes I can see so far blow my mind. I now embody a self I am so proud to be. And regardless of whether this leap "succeeds" or "fails," my gratitude for the journey is off the charts.

This ending isn't exactly an ending, but instead another stone on the pathway of my journey and, more likely than not, another beginning to my next leap.

I invite you to be present in your now while creating your future. Celebrate every win. Laugh every chance you get. Say "yes" to creating your vision. Show up to transform into that magical butterfly again and again and again.

I give you permission to leap.

But more importantly … do you?

Glossary of Terms

Abundance: the state or condition of having a copious quantity of something. Living with an abundance mindset means believing there is more than enough of everything to go around–for everyone.

Closed Energy: being in a position, belief, or mindset which blocks Universal Energy from entering your Physical and/or Spiritual World(s).

Comfort Zone: a psychological state in which things feel familiar to a person. When a person is in their comfort zone, they are at ease and in control of their environment, experiencing low levels of anxiety and stress. It is a place where a steady level of performance is possible. The comfort zone is a place where we stay to avoid any anticipated pain or discomfort in the future.

Daily Practice: a regular and consistent opportunity to connect with the Spiritual World to find guidance, give gratitude, and experience peace.

Ego: the part of the mind that mediates between the conscious and the unconscious and is responsible for developing and maintaining our sense of personal identity, self-esteem, and self-importance.

Faith: the act of having trust or confidence in someone or something without waiting for evidence. This term can often be associated with religion, however for the purposes of this book it does not have religious connotations.

Fight or Flight: a primitive physiological reaction that occurs in response to a perceived harmful event, attack, or threat to survival.

Financial Freedom: See abundance.

Foundation: the basis or groundwork upon which your life rests.

Glass Ceiling: an upper limit to professional advancement that is imposed upon women, minorities, and other non-dominant groups and is not readily perceived or openly acknowledged. Individuals can also have self-imposed glass ceilings which are upper limits defined by our own self-image.

Grounding: the practice of centering yourself within your body and connecting to the energy of the Earth. The easiest way to do this is to put your bare feet on the Earth by sitting in the grass with the soles of your feet on the ground.

Imposter Syndrome: a persistent feeling of inadequacy despite external proof otherwise.

Inner Naysayer: the voice in your head that judges, demeans, and generally bullies you into staying in your comfort zone. This is our brain's way of bringing us back to our comfort zone and out of perceived danger.

Inspired action: an action that comes naturally, sometimes spontaneously, and often straight from the Spiritual World.

Intention: a clear, positive statement aiming towards an outcome you desire to experience or create

Law of Attraction: a Universal principle that explains how each of us attract into our lives the things, circumstances, and experiences that align with our dominant and habitual thoughts and beliefs. It is often explained as, "like attracts like."

Leap: To leap is to attempt something whose existence or outcome cannot be proven. The desire to leap is often marked by either a deep unsettling discomfort, indicating the circumstances you find yourself in are not right, or by an inner knowing there is more available to you than your current reality. Examples of leaps: quitting a job, leaving a relationship, starting a business, relocation, changing careers, writing a book, etc.

Manifestation: the process of creating your reality by turning your thoughts into things.

Open Energy: being in a position, belief, or mindset to allow Universal Energy to enter your Physical and/or Spiritual World(s).

Physical World: one end of the Physical World/Spiritual World spectrum. This side is where we experience the human aspect of ourselves. These are the things we can see and touch such as: situations, circumstances, experiences, jobs, people, etc.

Soul Connection: a relationship with yourself that brings about the growth of your soul

Source or Spirit: a divine creator, higher power, or deity that exists, has existed, and will always exist (used interchangeably with God, Universe, or higher power)

Soul: the nonphysical part of a person that is the seat of our emotions and character.

Spiritual World: one end of the Physical World/Spiritual World spectrum. This side is where we experience the things we cannot see or touch, such as: faith, trust, magic, synchronicity, energy, etc.

Stages of Competence: a psychological learning model relating to the states involved in the process of progressing from incompetence to competence in a skill.

Universal Energy: This has been discussed and studied for centuries. It has been referred to as Chi, Prana, and Ki. It is an invisible energy that is present in all things existing in our Physical and Spiritual Worlds. It connects all planets, people, animals, plants, etc.

Vision Board: a tool used to help clarify, concentrate, and maintain focus on a specific life goal. Oftentimes a combination of words and images meant to direct and align your attention and feelings with your future.

Zone of Genius: this is your one-of-a-kind superpower you bring to the world. It's an area where you utilize your strengths to experience optimum satisfaction, impact, and potential.

Acknowledgements

First and foremost, I must thank Mama Seeley. As I write this, she's sitting beside me on an airplane, sleeping. This woman is beyond. Mama - you have been the fiercest protector, the loudest cheerleader, and even the most dedicated backstage fashion assistant. You have listened to me cry more than any mom should ever have to, and yet you never judge. I literally would not be the woman I am today without your guidance, encouragement, and even your boundaries. LU.

Next, this book would not have happened without the assistance of Jesse Tevelow and Simon Bogdanowicz. Your belief in me has been the only thing to keep me going on more days than I'd like to admit. Thank you for encouraging me, putting up with my high-achiever syndrome, and kicking me in the ass periodically (OK, OK, fine—frequently).

Also, massive love to Liz Von E. and Katie Soy. You were the first to read this book and the first to show me how powerful it could be in the world. Thank you for challenging me, asking me the hard questions, and encouraging me to "show, not tell."

To Naveen, whose belief in me has immeasurably shifted my mindset and, in turn, my ability to believe in myself. I am eternally grateful for your wisdom and friendship.

To my inner circle, I wouldn't have made it this far in life without you. Holy shit, you all keep me so sane.

To Marvin, Makayla, Dot and Jim, getting to this point in life has been filled with more highs and lows than any of us should ever experience. I have done it so imperfectly, so messily and so ungracefully. Yet you have been there in spite of it all. Thank you for your love (especially the tough love) and safety you've given me. I am a better woman because of each of you.

To my interns who were with me during this particular leap: Katie, Katie, Liz, and Cristina. Thank you for all your hard work and support. And I'm sorry I cried so much in front of you. I hope you learned some great, valuable lessons to take into the world for your future leaps.

Last, but not least, thank you to all my clients. Thank you for putting your trust in me to guide you and support you. Thank you for your vulnerability. Thank you for saying "yes" to your vision. Thank you for being brave enough to leap. I love you.

About the Author

Bri Seeley is an Inspirational Woman, Author, Life Coach and Speaker who supports women around the world to turn their inner visions into their outer realities.

Bri is motivated by a deeply held belief that every woman deserves to live a life that inspires her, and her work reflects this deep remembering of the possibility—nay, inevitability—that our desires hold.

Through her signature six-month training Permission to Leap (plus upcoming book + podcast by the same name!) she will guide you through the process of leaping from the day you commit to your vision, all the way through each stage, up until the day you land softly on the other side of it all.

A catalyst, speaker, and author, she is a regular contributor to *The Huffington Post* and *Influencive* and is known by many for her compassionate, yet tell-it-like-it-is guidance that creates massive and epic changes in every woman she encounters.

Bri has been featured on *Today, Forbes, Medium, Kickstarter, PBS, and Free Enterprise.*

References

Blakeley, Kiri. 2010. "Don't Trust Your Gut." Forbes (June 9). https://www.forbes.com/2010/06/09/oprah-winfrey-talk-show-auditions-own-network-forbes-woman-time-gut-intuition.html.

Bonabeau, Eric. 2003. "Don't Trust Your Gut." *Harvard Business Review* (May). https://hbr.org/2003/05/dont-trust-your-gut.

Dominican University of California. "Study Focuses on Strategies for Achieving Goals, Resolutions." Dominican University of California. https://www.dominican.edu/dominicannews/study-highlights-strategies-for-achieving-goals

Greer, Mark. 2005. "When intuition misfires." *American Psychological Association* 36, no. 3 (March): 58. http://www.apa.org/monitor/mar05/misfires.aspx.

Lally, Phillippa, Cornelia H.M. van Jaarsveld, Henry W.W. Potts, and Jane Wardle. 2010. "How are habits formed: Modelling habit formation in the real word." *European Journal of Social Psychology* 40, no. 6 (October): 998-1009.

Larré, K., McFarland, G., and Weaver, M. (2014, June). An Amazing Interview with Dr. Joe Dispenza. *Truly Alive Magazine.* http://www.trulyalive.net/amazing-interview-dr-joe-dispenza/

Lufityanto, Galang, Chris Donkin, and Joel Pearson. 2016. "Measuring Intuition: Nonconscious Emotional Information Boosts Decision Accuracy and Confidence." *Psychological Science* 27, no. 5 (April 6): 622-634. https://doi.org/10.1177/0956797616629403.

MacKinnon, J.B. 2016. "The Strange Brain of the World's Greatest Solo Climber." *Nautilus* (August 11). http://nautil.us/issue/39/sport/the-strange-brain-of-the-worlds-greatest-solo-climber.

MacMillan, Amanda. 2014. "5 Weird Ways Stress Can Actually Be Good for You." *Time* (August 22). http://time.com/3162088/5-weird-ways-stress-can-actually-be-good-for-you/.

Neureiter, Mirjam, and Eva Traut-Mattausch. 2016. "Inspecting the Dangers of Feeling like a Fake: An Empirical Investigation of the Imposter Phenomenon in the World of Work." Frontiers in Psychology (September 27). https://doi.org/10.3389/fpsyg.2016.01445.

Polman, Evan, Rachel L. Ruttan, and Joann Peck. 2016. "Using Curiosity to Increase the Choice of 'Should' Options." *American Psychological Association* (August). https://www.apa.org/news/press/releases/2016/08/using-curiosity.pdf

Ranganathan, Vinoth K., Vlodek Siemionow, Jing Z. Liu, et al. 2004. "From mental power to muscle power—gaining strength by using the mind." Neuropsychologia 42, no. 7: 944-956. https://doi.org/10.1016/j.neuropsychologia.2003.11.018

Sanders, Charles W., Mark Sadoski, Kim van Walsum, et al. 2008. "Learning basic surgical skills with mental imagery: using the simulation centre in the mind." *Medical Education* 42, no. 6 (June): 607-612. https://doi.org/10.1111/j.1365-2923.2007.02964.x

Yerkes, Robert M., and John D. Dodson. 1908. "The relation of strength of stimulus to rapidity of habit-formation." *The Journal of Comparative Neurology and Psychology* 18 (November): 459-482. https://doi.org/10.1002/cne.920180503

PERMISS ON TO

THE SIX-PHASE JOURNEY TO BRING
YOUR VISION TO LIFE

Made in the USA
San Bernardino, CA
31 October 2017